IN SEARCH OF ME

A Journey to Self-Love, Self-Worth & Purpose

Revised Edition of "The Journey To Uncover The Real Me 2018

By: Lynette M Bradshaw

In Search of Me

A Journey to Self-Love, Self-Worth & Purpose

Revised Edition of "The Journey To Uncover The Real Me 2018

By: Lynette M Bradshaw

Restore Her Worth

Before you turn the pages, I want you to know you are beginning a transformational, brave journey. Every step we take to heal, grow and elevate in our life, requires movement. You are in ACTIVATION mode as you turn these pages.

I have created a complimentary toolkit for you as a thank you for purchasing, "In Search of Me" and as an additional tool for you to listen to as you working out or driving in your car.

Claim your audios here: http://bit.ly/InSearchofMeToolKit

Don't forget to use the hashtags #InSearchofMe2018 and #InSearchofMeNow on social media. I look forward to hearing about what God does in your life after reading, "In Search of Me."

Pick up a copy of the companion Workbook- (In Search of Me-Workbook) and Moments of Gratitude-Journal for In Search of Me at www.Amazon.com or www.RestoreHerWorth.com

Don't forget to leave a review on Amazon!!

THIS BOOK IS DEDICATED TO

First and foremost, I dedicate this book to Jesus Christ, my Lord and Savior. Without God my breakthrough would not have been possible. I am grateful for Your Unconditional Love that brought me to myself. Thank you

To my children Jarrius, Derrick, Adriel and Charity, You are my heart and I am grateful that you were the first to teach me to love and to know that I could be loved. Each of you bring something different to my life, my heart & my soul. I will forever treasure and love you with all that is within me…

Thank you all for walking with me along my journey

Lynette M. Bradshaw

Table of Contents

Let Us Pray Before We Begin

Father God,

I thank you for the opportunity to share my journey, my heart and the lessons learned as You walked me through the process of Self-Discovery. I am so grateful You can now use all I have endured to heal, restore and renew your daughters. I pray for each person reading these pages. I pray that she has the faith and courage to go in search of herself underneath the pain, shame and silence that hides her voice, her power and her purpose.

In Jesus name, Amen

INTRODUCTION

We can live a lifetime searching the world and waiting for that special person or persons to come into our lives and give us the love that our souls long for and deserve. This search doesn't begin as we become adults, but it begins in our early childhoods. We are created in love because God is love. However, our parents are our first understanding of love. Depending on their upbringing, desire and knowledge of love, they can give us the true image of love or they present to us an illusion of what they believe to be love.

What happens if, as children we aren't given the assurance that we are loved, wanted and valued? What happens when all those around us only speak words that say love but show actions that speak hatred? One can become confused with what love really means. Our soul becomes hungry for what should come naturally to us as children. We know we are missing something, but as children how can we possibly be able to understand or vocalize that love is missing from our heart? We begin to feel that there is something wrong with us because even those near and dear to us don't see our presence as needed or appreciated. The wounds inflicted upon us through words and actions as children inflict the oozing wounds that will be the foundation we live from as adults. Children grow up to carry those wounds of insecurity, self-doubt, fear that they're not enough, and fear of rejection into adulthood. The hurt and pain begins infecting every relationship that they have. We look for others to validate {to give approval to, to confirm} us. We have a strong need for others to show and tell us that we are loved. We need others to show us that we are worth something because we don't love ourselves. We don't even know the meaning of self-love. With each intimate relationship or friendship during our search for love, we lose a very important person- ourselves. We work so hard to find someone to fill the voids of our childhood. We become a walking mask of illusion and lose our authentic self because we have become whoever we needed to be in order for others to approve of us, love us and stay with us. Some women spend all their lives searching for love and acceptance. She has lost her sense of worth in the shuffle of life. Others see a woman all together, but she is still the wounded child. She is still crying in the darkness hoping someone will look closer and listen deeper to her cries. The child within her is crying out in the darkness of her soul.

There is an end to the madness of the search and it begins with God. God is love. He is the Teacher and Giver of love. He is the One who created each of us in love. When we begin to open our heart to God, we can stop searching for the love we have longed for because God is here to restore us. He is here to find the lost little girl and mature her into the woman He created her to be, in His Image. The little girl within will know her cries are heard as God begins to comfort her, embrace her and assure her, He knows who she is. In the center of all the lies in our soul, is the authentic person we are called to be. You have felt lost in the wilderness of your own life. You have felt lost and without identity in a large world. You have cried out from within the wounds of your soul. It is time to find yourself, your true self, and to begin to love you for who you are. First you have to discover what love really is and then apply it to your wounds. You no longer have to walk around under a mask and wonder why your life is filled with disappointment and pain. The answers to the many questions are within you in Christ Jesus. The real you is hidden under the person you believed you had to become to receive any form of love.

Everyone's journey is different. Everyone's wounds are different. The one thing that is comparable is that we have to come to the end of who we were told to be, who we thought we had to be and who we think we are before we see the beauty of who we really are. God is here to walk with you step by step. Your wounds do not have to continue to ooze and infect your life. You can be free. You can be whole. You can begin to love you.

You can discover who you really are. The love you have searched so long for has been available to you, but you didn't know. From childhood to adulthood, the thirst deep within you can be quenched. What you have to give to the world is too valuable to withhold. This is why it is important to pull off the masks that have covered your true identity. Underneath the scars, the anger, the rage and fear is a child crying, "Someone love me." God is here to answer that call. He has heard your cries and felt your pain. His love for His children will fill every hurt and wound completely. The love our heart and soul deserves is available. Our search for love and understanding God is love will help us to discover ourselves.

CHAPTER 1

The Journey

> *"For I know the plans I have for you," declares the Lord. 'plans to prosper you and not harm you, plans to give you hope and a future."*
> (Jeremiah 29:11).

L ife is a journey within itself. Even in my mother's womb, I was on a journey to live. The nine months within her were the beginning of many years of pain, heartache and disappointment. Walking through daily routines, one can lose sight of the fact that with each passing moment he or she is being molded, formed, strengthened, broken and renewed. We tend to see life as a series of normal days. At what point in life do we ever stop and look into the eyes that are staring back at us in the mirror? At what point do we look into those eyes and say, "Who are you really?"

In order to move forward, it is necessary to look back and see where you started, examine what you have done, and accept where you are at this very moment. The thought of doing this may feel paralyzing as the thoughts of your current life and past pain begin to flow in your mind. I came to a point in my life where my mind was constantly racing with all that had taken place in my life. There were days when I wanted to scream and say, "God are you listening?" There were days I wondered if God cared what I was going through. Even in those hours, there was always a flicker of hope.

I often thought to myself that this had to be someone else's life because surely it could not be mine. Although the journey has been mind-blowing and confusing, I have to say along the way I have found the person who was hidden underneath pain, shame and silence. I have found someone who had been lost for so long. Somewhere deep in the crevices of my soul, was a person who came to the end of what she knew as herself to begin new.

For me this journey started in 2010, when I decided to get a divorce after four children and almost eighteen years of marriage. Since then, my life has seemed to be in roller coaster mode with all the twists and turns of life. There were many days of wondering what caused me, at this stage of life, to feel like I was in total control but somehow without control of my life? My emotions, my thoughts, my ideas, my spiritual and natural sight were changing. I was in a new place within myself. I had no idea where this strange road would take me, but ready or not, my journey had begun. What felt like me losing my mind, was actually the shifting of all the old things (thoughts, words, ideas, fears, pain) within me to make room for the newness that God was bringing me into. When things shift, one becomes unsteady. Well, it is no different when God says it is time for one to walk into the person they were ordained to be. It is not comfortable. It is scary. It leaves the individual unstable. Yet, it is necessary in order to give birth to one's destiny. The twists and turns on my journey were the labor pains. Unknowingly, I was in the birthing position to give birth to what God purposed for my life.

The journey has been filled with hurt, weakness, anger, self-doubt, needing love, low self-esteem and no self-love. The journey has many questions and few answers. I somehow know that those questions are warranted, and they won't always remain. I am here now. I am on the other side of divorce. I am reveling in questions but I can't give up no matter how I scream inside. This journey is one I never thought I would take, and it makes me wonder how I got here. What changed within me after all these years? Where did the strength come from and what caused the switch to change?

I felt something strange inside of me. I was starting to stand up for myself more but felt frustrated doing so. I strongly objected to receiving the same treatment that for years I accepted as okay. I felt strong and weak in the same breath; however, the deepest emotion I felt was fear. I was afraid of what was happening to me. The love I was starting to feel for myself felt strange. I had never loved myself because I did not know how to love me. The road to loving yourself when you never have can be scary and confusing. However, that road is what brought me to this place. Life, as beautiful as it is, has so many turns and detours. When you find yourself at a place where you always longed to be and yet never knew how to get there, it can feel like you are dreaming. What I realized is this dream was always meant to be my reality and I believe it is yours also. No longer do you have to sit on the sidelines of your own life and be afraid to get in the game. "For God hath not given us the spirit of fear, but of power, and of love, and of a sound mind." (2 Timothy 1:7) No longer do you have to think about never being enough to step on the field. In fact, picking up this book, reading it and allowing yourself to believe you can begin again, is the beginning to your journey. Choosing to live beyond where you have been, is a power move.

I want to share my journey with you. I decided to take God's hand and walk with Him, step by step into a new life. While I write these words, my journey continues in the quest to discover me. The feeling of not knowing clearly what is going on in my life comes and goes, but I know God is with me. Yet, I can say with a certainty that God has grown me up from the little girl that decided she wanted and needed a divorce to the woman I am in this moment.

This is my story of how God allowed the end of a marriage to help me find what I had never had before, Self-Love and my true identity. This is my journey of how uncertainty and sometimes anger can be just enough to force you into realizing you are more than what you've believed. It is my journey to discover I am more powerful than I was made to feel. I deserved so much more and now I can have more. It is my self-discovery story.

This story tells of my realization that in order to know me or find me I would have to know God in a deeper way than ever before. Who I am is hidden in God. The love I desired and needed are in Him. In Him I was purposed to find me. My truth is hidden in His love.

The same goes for you. Everything you felt you lost can not stop you from stepping into your journey to receive what you have waited so long for, love. What you need is in God. Who you need, is in God. It is your time to walk your journey and exchange pain for hope.

What are you Feeling?

_____

_____

_____

_____

_____

_____

_____

_____

_____

CHAPTER 2

Unconditionally

"We love because He first loved us" (John 4:19).

As I sat and watched John Legend sing the song, "All of Me," which I had never heard before, on the Oprah show, my soul seemed to open up. What he sang about was just what my soul had searched for all my life. In that moment I realized that it was that type of Love that would totally heal every wound in my soul. As I replayed the song over and over again, I came to the understanding that although I wanted to share my heart and life with a man who loved me the way John Legend's song described, I would have to first accept that God already loves me this way. The song says, "Give me all of you." It describes the unconditional love he has for his love with all imperfections, the good and the bad of her. Nothing would stop him from giving her all of him. All he asked in return was that she gives him all of her. Tears swelled up from somewhere deep inside of me. This song made me reflect on a relationship I entered into after my divorce that had just ended after seventeen months. I thought the love that I wanted, needed and had come to realize I deserved all my life, had found me. Somewhere along the way, it fell apart. I also reflected on my marriage and how I searched for love within it for years. When I heard the song, I again began to think I would live my life without someone who would love me unconditionally and truthfully. It was only as I continued to listen to the song, that I realized God was saying to me, "This is how I love you."

Gods' love in that moment began to peel away the pain and disappointment of forty-six years of my life. My soul was being washed in the love of the One who first and forever loved me. I always knew God loves me, but I didn't KNOW He loves me. My life had made me repeatedly question who is this God the Father, God the lover of my soul, God the one who protects me? There were many times growing up and being an adult, I thought in my unspoken tongue, "How could God love me and allow me to endure so much?" Have you ever wondered the same thing? Have you ever doubted the love of God for you because of the pain you have gone through in life? Life, again, can bring us into a place where even if we see others feeling loved and powerful as they live their daily lives, we think, "God what about me?" Maybe you are like me. Maybe you always knew God loved you, but do you really know He loves you?

As far back as I looked upon my life's journey I only saw confusion and pain. While hearing the words of "All of Me" in that moment I felt an inner strength and love I never knew. I was at a new stage of the journey to find out who is Lynette Bradshaw. I felt myself screaming inside saying, "Who am I" and "What is going on with me right now?" Even though I saw myself in a different way I was still feeling misunderstood or was it just my perception? Either way, I felt those around me still saw the woman who did not know who she was, really. I felt they heard anger, when I was really learning to speak in a new way. I did not know how to show them at this time that I was changing, because I did not understand this all myself. This was a strange thought to me. Yet the thought also gave peace. To know for the first time in my life that love would be a part of my life was scary and exciting at the same time. Somehow, I knew if I gave all of me, that I would receive more than I could ever imagine. My heart was over filled with love that caused my soul to weep. I wanted to hold that moment in time for all eternity. The world seemed to stand still, and it was only God and me. Love had pierced my soul and I felt I could move forward. It was my understanding that I would feel this type of love from someone who looked at me and saw my brokenness, my hurt emotions, my broken heart and who would choose to love me unconditionally. The person who sees beyond your wounds is supposed to embrace you for you and still love you. I believed he would be my knight in shining armor who rushes in to save me. Thankfully God showed me that He was the one for whom I was waiting. There is no human being who could compare to the love I was feeling in Gods' presence. Through His love I could not only move forward but move forward boldly. Gods' love expands your heart to receive it and even then, over flows within you. It is beautiful how He used the words to the song, "All of Me," to express to me His love for me. He is the only One who could see my wounds and still love me in the way that my soul longed for. He is the white knight that came in to save and rescue me. He swept me off my feet and held me as a child who was lost in those moments. My tears flowed like a cleansing rain and made me new. Going forward no longer was an option but a necessity for me. I felt that I had a responsibility to give back all of me to the only One who I knew would give me all of Him through His love for me. I knew that I had to trust God with me in order to have the masks to fall to the ground and find the real me behind them. There was no stopping me anymore. Love found me and through it I would find me.

Are you hearing God sing to you in a way that you are trying to ignore? Maybe you do not realize He is speaking because it is unfamiliar. Maybe you have gone without true love for so long that it is easier to deny than risk embracing it, only to be disappointed. His love for you is like no other and will never disappoint and never leave (Hebrews 13:5b). The love of God for you is what you have searched for in so many and still came up empty. The sweet melody of God speaks to every cell within you and revives every place within that you believed could no longer live or feel love. It is in His love we discover who we are behind the mask. We pull down the walls through an unbreakable love affair with God. He is the only One who knows the rhythm of your heart. He will sing the perfect song to your broken places. Be still before Him in surrender and allow the beauty of His words to lift you, heal you and most importantly, reveal you to you. Those who came before were not in rhythm with your heartbeat. They could not speak the write words to speak to your heart. God has sent His word just for you. In His expression of love towards you, He will release, restore and revive the dry bones and set your feet a dancing.

What are you Feeling?

_____

_____

_____

_____

_____

_____

_____

_____

_____

CHAPTER 3

It's time

"To every thing there is a season and a time to every
purpose under heaven...a time to heal"
(Ecclesiastes 3:1:1-3a)

By the time of our divorce, my former husband and I had been married for twenty years. We had four beautiful children and a beautiful home. I never thought I would ever have the courage to stand up for myself and say no more ultimatums, no more counseling, no more anything. At what point did I cross that line and reach the breaking point? I didn't get there easily. I was confused. I was sad and I became depressed. What was I feeling? I started to think maybe I was down because my business was not producing a profit and to me, it seemed as if I had failed again. My daughter, whom I stayed home to raise from a newborn, was now in school full time. I didn't feel like I had a purpose anymore and I felt my mind was playing games on me.

In 2010, my life was no different from previous years. I was still hoping that my gift of photography would finally blossom into a prosperous business. I was getting up in the mornings and taking my two youngest children to school and coming back home. Somewhere along the way, I became overly angry and sad. I didn't understand what was going on with me, and I didn't like what I was feeling. I was reaching out from this place inside myself that was strange to me and so confusing. I was reaching for someone to help me understand what was happening to and in me without judgement. I was reaching out for someone to take me and hold me and say, "I am with you." "Many women would love the life I have," I thought to myself. To be able to stay home all day and work one's passion (my photography business) and then relax before the kids came home from school was a dream come true. However, the business wasn't doing what I had hoped it would do and it hadn't in seven years. I was feeling like nothing I ever tried worked for me. Things never seemed to work for me, but it seemed that others could go after a dream and it would explode. At least, that is what my mind told me and I believed it. I needed to feel like I could win at something, and I thought this was it. Being at home all day gave me a lot of time to let my mind wander. It gave me time to think about my life and where it was.

I had been a faithful wife for seventeen years to a man who just didn't hear me when I expressed how I was in pain.

The loneliness I felt in my marriage was unbearable. I felt he made me feel guilty for having feelings of not being loved by him because he was providing for our children and me by working and bringing in the money. My hurt turned into fear that I would live this life forever without feeling loved or wanted. The fear became frustration and rage. It had remained this way for years. Gradually, I began to feel that I needed more and deserved better. I tried to express to him that I was not happy as I had many times before. A deep sadness began to consume me. I talked to a friend about it and she gave me the words that as a Christian one should give. She said I needed to pray about it and ask God what to do. This was not the time to preach to me because I needed someone to hear my heart and allow me to be human. She asked me what was I looking for? I tried to explain it to her, but I felt she wasn't hearing the screams from my soul that said, "I don't know what I'm looking for but this is no longer it." I felt I was smothering within my own mind and no one could save me. I thought, surely, I must be going crazy because this can't be normal. I went about my day and life as normal just dragging myself along. What was it I was feeling? I didn't have any idea. My husband didn't seem to pay much attention to me. Couldn't he see that I was in distress? I don't know why I expected him to because he never could connect to me in that way.

It was in July of 2010, and I could feel that something had changed in me. Was I really saying to myself that I wanted a divorce? Where did that come from? Enough was enough. I had gone to my husband so many times before over the years and stressed to him that I was not happy in our relationship. I wanted him to know if we didn't work on our relationship we were not going to make it. He would go with the flow of seemingly trying to do better but I had come to know that it wouldn't last. Deep within my heart I felt it no longer mattered. Could I really say to him that I no longer wanted to be in relationship with someone who never loved me as his wife? Could I really tell him that there was no need for ultimatums or counseling because I was done? Surely not because the person I know me to be is not that strong. The person I knew as Lynette didn't love herself enough to think that she could step away from this relationship. Even though I was changing, there were still issues in me that were struggling to deeply accept that I deserved more. My mind was so confused. I remember saying to God, "I don't know how and I don't know why now, but I feel in my core that this is what I need to do for me." I was terrified. I can't tell you that I heard from God audibly telling me it was ok for me to get a divorce. However, I knew it was time for me.

The day I decided to tell Devon it was over was a day I felt like I was going into surgery of some kind and I didn't know if I would come out of it. Regardless, I felt the inner strength that I had never known before. That strength led me to believe I would pull through. As I sat across from my husband and told him that we needed to go our separate ways, I found myself talking out loud and at the same time quietly saying, "God help me please." I could feel him staring at me in disbelief. I told him that this was not like the other times where I was giving him an

27

ultimatum, but I was done. I told him this was not about him anymore but about me deserving better. I deserved to be loved. I told him that God was helping me to love myself and helping me to see that the marriage was no longer for me. I knew we loved each other but not the way that two people love each other when they are married. This was no longer acceptable. I was numb and shaking, but I had finally put into words what I had been feeling for so long and there was no turning back.

What conversations are you needing to have with the thought replaying in your mind, people or old wounds that you need to release? In the journey to uncover who you really are, there will be a separation and a divorce in order for you to move forward. You see, in order to reveal truth, we must be willing to let go and disengage with those people, thoughts and ideas of ourselves. Holding on to these things will only keep us stuck. The disconnect begins within first. It is a mental shift. It is an emotional shift. It is a heart shift. It is a soul shift. All the things that speak into your life daily, sometimes unknowingly, are the very things you must be willing to say, "No more."

What are you Feeling?

_____

_____

_____

_____

_____

_____

_____

_____

_____

CHAPTER *4*

The Foundation

"...being rooted and grounded in love"
(Ephesians3:17).

Why is love so important to me? It is important because I feel it has been withheld from me all my life. As a child and as an adult I was very insecure. I didn't have a voice because I was made to feel that my opinions did not matter. It seems that everyone I interacted with made me feel worse than the one before. Inside I was crying out, "Somebody love me and just like me, please." I realized as I began my relationship with God that it wasn't about me being a child that I went through so much, it was what Satan wanted to steal from me as an adult. As we go through life, we hardly find many people who will stop and take the time to invest in our lives and ask, "Why are you the way you are?" We act out of our pain, sometimes unknowingly.

Love is a masterful emotion. According to The Merriam Webster's Dictionary and Thesaurus, Masterful means having a domineering nature. God is love; however, until we discover God within ourselves, we search in others for that love. Often that search is in vain. If those in our lives who are expected to love us don't know how to love us because of their own wounds, we can begin to feel unworthy of love. As children our sense of self is formed. It is important that we receive love, affection, adoration, correction, comfort as well as discipline. It is also important we are given the opportunity to speak our opinions, concerns, fears and hopes.

When those around us are wounded, they take care of us from their wounds. They themselves are victims and we become victimized. At the time when self is supposed to evolve into its purpose, self denies itself because it is in shambles. Insecurity, shame, lack of confidence, lack of worth, lack of ability to do anything replaces the journey toward self-acceptance, self-worth, self-dignity, and self-love.

The road of our destiny was meant to be wrapped in God's love because God's love allows us to give birth to the self that was meant to walk in greatness. Instead, love was never on the scene. This is how I have felt most of my life. It is not fun living life being compared to strangers on the street, family members, and basically anyone who breathed. My journey has been one without a voice, without worth, without value and needing to be validated by someone. I knew about God as He was spoken of in church. However, it would be many years later before I realized in order for my pain to heal, I had to not only know God, but have a relationship with Him. I remember at a young age, within myself, I made the decision that I would do whatever it took to get love. Even at a young age I wanted someone to love me. It seemed that no one did. In my child-like mind, that could only mean I needed to do something otherwise I would never be loved. That decision would lead me down a road of more pain, deep pain. God never meant for me to look outside of myself for love and validation.

What I needed was always within me, in Him. He was there when I made that decision, and He was there when I was hurt and betrayed by others. God was there when my search for love caused disappointment time and time again. The road I chose was chosen because I was in pain. When one is in pain, he or she hungers for it to go away and will do whatever is necessary to take it away, even if it is a temporary release. This is why many times, we seek out substitute healers such as sex, shopping, gambling, multiple degrees and more, because they distract us from feeling the pain and numbs us temporarily. Seeking a substitute will slowly, but surely, deepen the pain we are already trying to avoid. The truth is, unless one goes to God, who is love, he or she won't find the love that surely takes away every heartache and disappointment. My desperate search for love gave way to something far worse. It gave way to shame, unbearable pain, the loss of my worth and the loss of my dignity (a sense of pride in oneself; self-respect). It would take many years to begin the process to regain it. The good news is that it was never truly gone. It was just lying dormant inside of me, waiting for me to desire it again and come searching for it.

The devil made sure I kept searching for love in people who were wounded themselves, therefore, wounding me. You see our wounds attract wounded people. We recognize each other through our brokenness. They may be a couple steps ahead of you. They may have mastered hiding their wounds better than you, but they are still wounded. Our lovers lie with us and feed the inner turmoil of insecurity, fear, doubt, self-sabotage and hopelessness. These wounded lovers had no idea they were major players in the plan Satan set for me. They were representatives of temporary solutions to take away my inner war to love myself. Sadly, at the time, I was visually impaired in my spirit and could not recognize our wounds wrestled with each other. They had no idea the parts they would play in inflicting wounds within my soul that would take many years to heal. They had no idea they were teaching me to hate myself moment by moment. Funny how the search for love turned on me because what I searched for, and who I searched for it in, caused me to hate the person I was. Wasn't my search supposed to bring love? Where was the love? Where was the love for me? I was supposed to feel better but I didn't. In fact, I felt worse. I was losing myself because each time my soul was wounded, a little piece of my core existence was dying away. Just because one receives the words "I love you" doesn't mean they are receiving authentic love. Just because someone says the right words doesn't mean it is love. For every act of hatred toward me, clothed in an imitation of love, my soul was building a wall and creating a place within me that became dry as bones without flesh. My heart became a prison of rooms that held the wounds, the residue, and the expectations I believed love would bring to me.

Satan's plan was to not only destroy a little girl but to take the voice, the worth and value of a woman. The wounds inflicted upon a child are not really about the child herself, but about the woman who is purposed for greatness in God. It is that woman who will speak to multitudes and cause them to know their value and worth and to have her own voice given by God. Satan came to steal that through every blow placed upon my soul that inflicted a wound. Those wounds took my voice to speak of my value and worth. They stole my identity and said I had nothing worth saying that anyone wanted to hear. Yet, I had much to do and say for God. He gave me a voice. He gave me worth. He gave me value, and I would have to be restored years later in order to walk into my destiny. I am walking into it.

What are you Feeling?

_____

_____

_____

_____

_____

_____

_____

_____

CHAPTER *5*

The Cry

"I cried unto the LORD with my voice; with my voice unto the LORD did I make my supplication"
(Psalm 142:1).

The cry for help from a broken woman comes from deep within. She cries not only for the woman she has become but the little girl broken inside of her. The little girl is broken at the point of her decision to search for the love that seemed to run away from her. I came to a place in life where I realized I couldn't stop the hurt on my own. The reality that I was shielded with masks hit home. Sadly, I didn't know who this person was staring back at me in the mirror. Looking back from the mirror were eyes that showed pain but I wore a smile that said, "I am ok." The mask that I had worn since childhood was cracking and crumbling before me. Piercing through the cracks of the masks was someone who was lost and needed to be found.

Yet, I didn't believe anyone could come and find me after all this time. Friends and lovers who came behind the mask inflicted more pain and made me crumble and fold into a fetal position inside myself. Those I considered lovers would continue the cycle of betrayal, lies and deception. Those who were friends only wanted to be heard, but never listened. In doing so, wounds were deepened and inflicted. The person under the mask was so wounded and bleeding she didn't know where to apply the bandages anymore.

Eventually, you come to a place where you ask yourself, "Why don't others like me?" Aren't I nice? Aren't I a Christian? Didn't I put on the right mask at the right time to fool them into thinking I wasn't insecure or jealous of them? Didn't I put on my best dress that says, "See me please?" When I reached the point in life where I looked behind the mask and became afraid of what I saw, something had to change.

I remember one day saying a simple prayer to God. This prayer was the most honest prayer of help I had ever said at that point in my life. Even then I wasn't sure anyone would answer. My prayer was, "God help me." There was no way God was listening to me, I told myself. He had become The God I heard preachers and others speak of in church. The unseen spirit of God that I hoped was there when I prayed, but honestly wasn't sure He listened to me. The prayer was said and the rebellious child inside of me said, "He won't hear you because He never did before when we cried to him to stop the pain." The same rebellious little girl that had ceased to grow beyond the point of my hurt and decision to find love, was still speaking within me.

How could she still have so much power inside of me? I was looking at the woman in the mirror. However, what I needed to do was see the hurt little girl crying out of my soul. I never imagined that simple prayer would start many years of war within my soul. The war was between the past, the present and the pull toward my destiny. I did not have a clue what I would have to endure to get to a place of just feeling sane.

When we reach out to God to save us from our pain, Satan won't just take his hands off our lives and release us easily. We have to fight our way out through prayer. I wanted my pain to cease, but wanting it wasn't enough. The fight for my soul had begun. The good news was The One who the rebellious child within me said wouldn't be there was The One carrying me. My cry for help was out of desperation and pain. How can one person hurt so much and no one around them care enough or pay enough attention to see them in pain? The reality of being broken in your spirit and heart is that you become so good at wearing masks. Sometimes we hide the brokenness from all those who look upon our face. The skill to put on the right mask for the right person and situation was how I learned to cope in life. No matter how you put it, it was manipulation. Manipulating others to see me, to like me, to hear me and acknowledge that I existed was covered under many masks. At least I *thought* the masks covered me well. Truth is, we may believe we are hiding securely underneath the mask we wear, but others see past it. We are really only manipulating ourselves from our own truth. It is painful to accept, but the truth is, insecurity, fear, deception, lying, pain, anger, bitterness shows up when we show up. The pain becomes our personal brand. Our brand, just like in business, says "This is who I am or who I believe I am." It says, "I am not sure of myself but I want others to believe I have it all together. We wear the pain on our sleeve and bite those viscously who attempt to call us out on our unspoken reality.

My cry to God came from a broken child filled with anger, insecurity, fear, doubt and someone needing to exhale. At this point I felt I couldn't breathe or exhale. I was only existing and walking around feeling like the world was moving and I was standing still. Did anyone really see me? My emotions were from one extreme to the other. They vacillated from sadness, anger, joy and rage. "What is wrong with me?" This thought would come to me so many times. I thought I was crazy and without any understanding. I just wanted it to stop and go away. I had children and a husband, a good job, a nice home, my health and strength. Shouldn't I be happy? One would think that having those blessings I would be great. However, the things on the outside couldn't do anything for a broken spirit and heart. I required something much deeper to make me feel complete and happy. Happiness was an unfamiliar emotion. I had never been happy. I didn't understand what being happy meant. The story of my childhood had rolled over into every corner of my life. I was still searching for affirmation, for love, for approval, for someone to say that I'm not a mistake and my life is more than what I see.

God are you listening? Did you hear my outcry? Are you coming? I walked away from that prayer not really believing anything good would happen for me or any good would come of it. I'm not sure what I was expecting. Whatever it was it didn't seem to be coming fast enough, if at all. My rebellious alter ego was used to having her way and she would act out when she didn't get her way. The spirit of rebellion had been one of many defenses that carried me through life. You have heard the saying, "act your age," right? Even though I was in my late 20's, I was acting like a nine-year-old child. I didn't realize what was going on. Being a grown up didn't stop the childish behavior-the pouting, acting jealous of other women's relationships, and smothering anyone who gave me any attention. Sometimes we look at adults who we believe they are behaving in a childish manner and don't really understand or stop to consider why they are acting the way they do. It takes someone with a spiritual heart for God's people to see beyond the flesh and see the heart and soul of that person. I am reminded of someone who God allowed to see me just this way without judgment. Her name is Louise. Ms. Louise was a member of my former church. She was a woman who taught me so many things and embraced me with love even though I resisted her. She grabbed your attention with her natural height, probably 5' 11 to 6 feet, but she captivated your attention with her powerful love for you. She would tell me, "You want love but when someone tries to give it to you, you go the other direction." She was right. I ran from what I needed and wanted because it was easier and it felt protected. I felt protected in running because it was easier than the risk of being rejected. In all truth, I felt unworthy of love and when others tried to give it to me, I avoided them. How could she see me in my true state of brokenness? Who is this woman? Can she really be real? The little girl in me showed up in my body language and my facial expressions but Ms. Louise never turned away from me. Although there were many times when she would simply just let me be, she never turned her back on me. What I discovered on my journey is this important truth, God protects us all. He would allow others to love me, embrace me, teach me, speak to my spirit, but His love for them would pull them back when my rebellious nature sought to bring hurt to them. Yes, it made me feel the familiar abandonment. Yes, it made feel the familiar stabbing pain of feeling unwanted. I couldn't understand why He would pull away from me what I needed. As I began to heal, I had to face the truth that God does not want any of His children hurt, abused and mistreated. This includes His children He releases to serve us in our time of pain. The rebellious spirit of the little wounded girl within me acted out because being rebellious was my shield. Sometimes we unintentionally block what we prayed for when it actually shows up because it is unfamiliar. We will do whatever we have to in order to not feel pain again. Ms. Louise was who I needed at a desperate and low time in my life. She saw me, she really saw me and that terrified me. The spirit of God within her saw me for who I was within, a broken and battered innocent little girl with a hunger to be loved. Her words show up in my life even today. I find myself sharing with others the lessons I learned from her. She has gone on to heaven and her words still help to heal me. They remind me God still hears my cry and He still sends help. Rest in Heaven Ms. Louise, I will never forget you.

Too many times we look at others and judge how they act and not care enough to ask the question, "Why?" I remember thinking, how was I supposed to nurture my children being a hurting child myself? I was doing it, but not successfully, which made me feel worse. Desperately I wanted to give them what I didn't have, LOVE. I have always felt my children are the greatest blessing to me. I wanted them to look at their mom and be proud of me, feel loved and adored. Because of the pain I was living in, I could not see I was giving what I was given because it was all I knew. God had blessed me with three sons and a precious daughter to rear, but I felt like I wasn't giving them the mother they deserved. My deep pain was doing just the opposite. The victim was making them victims. God did you hear me? Where are you? I need help because these masks are cracking and I'm falling apart. Help me………………

Did God really hear my cry? Did He see my mask falling that I had depended on all my life in order to live this life of pain? "God, where are you?" This was my pain cry. I needed God in those moments as I was being stripped of everything I considered a shield for me. Everything that was comfort for me, was now cracking at the seams. God, I need your help, NOW! This is a S.O.S. from your daughter. God, I am searching for me and I don't know what to do in this turmoil in my mind. God, You hear me right? Yes, I knew God heard me. It did not feel good, but I somehow knew God heard my cry. I knew I could not turn away nor run away.

I made a conscious decision that the fear of what was ahead of me, outweighed the pain I felt I was dying in.

What are you Feeling?

CHAPTER *6*

God Sends Help

"In my distress I cried unto the LORD, and he heard me" (Psalm 120:1).

Here I am many years later realizing my cry to God is still being answered. I didn't realize my healing wouldn't manifest all at once. God had to pull back many layers of pain, heartache, doubt, insecurity, hate, and guilt to find the person who was broken, shattered and needing His Love. Over the years He has continued to answer my call. Sometimes I feel I'm still the broken soul in some areas of my life. Now I have a greater understanding and deeper relationship with the One who not only heard but answered my cry for help. God sends Help when we call.

My pain began at a young age when my father, who lived in our home, was emotionally disconnected to me. My mother said words that only made me feel unwanted, unloved, unneeded and we did not seem to connect with each other. When I made the decision to search for love and attention, it was because I was lacking it in my home. In order to fill the places within me where the love I needed from my parents should have been, I needed to cry out to God to fill me and hear me. This lack in them, caused me to lack. Even though they gave, it was not what I needed to feel loved and wanted. The lack created emptiness. The emptiness could only be filled through God's love for me and in me. As a child, you do not realize how the trauma of being emotionally abandoned will show up in your adult life. As a child, you do not understand that your parents are to be your protectors and your example of love. Yet, as you begin to feel the emptiness, even as a young person, you can do what I did and make an inner decision to search for something to fill it. Because of my relationship with my mom, I would see other women with their daughters and feel jealous of their relationship because I did not have this. I would see little girls with their dads and long for my dad to see me as his precious little girl, even as an adult. What I was meant to have, I did not have. I searched. I hungered for what I would later discover was rightfully mine, love. Even though I knew God would help His children, but what about me? Would God help me or abandon me emotionally and mentally, the way my dad did? Would God beat me down with His words the way my mom did? Many times I thought the answers to those questions would be yes, but I discovered His love for me and His words for me would heal every wound inflicted.

Are we willing to accept His help and allow it to be sufficient even when the pain of healing seems unbearable? Allowing God's Love to heal our broken places is an act of courage and sacrifice. It requires us releasing ourselves into His hands one piece at a time, if need be. Do those words frighten you? To think you can release the broken pieces of who you are to God, one layer at a time, when you may feel you do not even know if you can, can be terrifying. They frightened me. Would God turn away from me the way others did? The mind can tell you He will, but His love for us is greater than anyone we have encountered on our journey. Trust me when I tell you, you are safe releasing yourself to Him. I was so broken when I cried out to God. I felt I was at the end of all I knew to do to stop hurting. I didn't know who I was. I didn't know why I hurt so deeply. I didn't know how to make the pain go away. I didn't know it would take what I so desperately craved, Love, to heal me. Not the love of a natural man or natural mother and father, but the Love of My Heavenly Father. He sent what would cut through the broken and wounded places, His Love, and illuminated the light of healing in my soul. We have used what we knew about love as our healing method. The problem is we couldn't understand what love was because we have lived life searching for someone or something to fill up the empty places within us. Sometimes we take the right words with the wrong actions, as love. Sometimes we can believe if we act good enough, do the right thing or be the right person, then the love we hunger for, will show up. Yet, when we are hurting, we lose our ability to know and understand love. We are misguided. This leads us into friendships and relationships that are toxic. Even when someone really wants to give us true love in relationships, we can possibly suffocate that love. We push people away and then we feel abandoned and blame them for leaving. It is hard for us to see our actions and accept the consequences of being needy. Some people will hang in there with us and try and show us a new sense of love because they care about us, but soon it can become too much for them to carry. God will allow them to walk away in order for them not to be wounded.

I'm so grateful for God having patience with me. He loves me in such special ways. My soul is refreshed coming into the truth that God loves me and has loved me all my life. My heart leaps as I think of God, the creator of all things, loving me. All those years of pain brought me to my knees and He brought me to my feet. God is always listening to us when we pray. He hears our hearts tears and the cry of our soul. He promised He would never forsake us according to Hebrews 13:5. Sometimes when the pain is so grave and cutting to the heart and soul, we can't say a word audibly. Even in our tears, God speaks our language. The moment we say Amen, we have to believe it is done.

Life can become exhausting when someone tries to fix themselves, without God. God is a gentle God and He will not push His way into our lives. The moment I said God help me, my life began to transform. However, I still was looking at my life and God through the same sick eyes I had prior to praying to God. In doing so, I thought nothing was changing. What I did not realize was everything was changing. My foundation, my excuses, my beliefs, my outlook, my heart and my mind were all being shaken and rebuilt, one piece at a time. The things around me were not changing yet because they were not supposed to._Pain is within but it manifests itself in our lives. Healing has to take place within before the evidence of it is seen. Healing is painful, and sometimes the pain is so hard we give up before our complete healing takes root. Imagine having an old scar on your skin that looks healed. When you remove a piece of the scab you see an oozing wound underneath. As you begin to peel back more of the scab, the oozing worsens and the pain is the same as the day you injured it. This is the same way the wounds of our soul are. We have covered up our pain with sex, one relationship after another, food, shopping, drugs, alcohol and many other natural things that will delay us in dealing with our wounds. The substitutes we use for God's Word will never allow healing. They will only scab over the deep wounds underneath. The more we use substitutes, the deeper the wounds become. Like the wounds on our skin, once we begin to peel back the layers, the pain is still there. It is as fresh as when it was inflicted. God is our healer {Exodus 15:26). He is waiting for His children to cry out to Him in prayer and worship, "Help me."

The masks can only remain so long before they begin to crumble. The truth is the mask only hides a person from themselves. As I began to heal, I was embarrassed when I realized how others saw me. It became clear why people didn't like me or didn't want me around them. I was a ticking time bomb with explosive emotions. I realized that all those years I assumed I was protected behind my masks, I was actually vulnerable to those wanting to use me. I was vulnerable also to those who would abuse me and those who didn't care to ask why you are the way you are. My shields were not really shields at all. They were an illusion of protection for me. Accepting the truth of how others saw me in my broken state, took a toll on me. Accepting that I was who they saw took a long time. Shame came to me like a flood as my mind reminded me of those I had encountered. My face flushed with the thought that other people could look at me and see the total opposite I believed I was showing them in order for them to embrace me. How could I not see what they saw? How could I be this up and down person? How could I be so jealous? My scabs had fallen off and now it was time to deal with the flesh beneath them. The steps to healing are a process. Accepting God's love is a process. There are steps to each but when the pain becomes too much, we want to skip the steps needed in front of us in order to leap to the feel-good stage. Isn't that why we use substitutes in our life? Isn't that why we cover the wounds and pour substances into our body that bring a numbness, but a good feeling, if only temporarily? It is easier to use something that is only lasting for the moment, because we can detach from it and ignore what is there even when it is toxic to our life. The steps to healing were almost like the steps to love. God would use the pain in those wounds to bring my healing. I never considered the pain because I was thinking I could bypass it and get to the feel-good moments. Just like the wounds inflicted to the skin, there is a time for the pain, the scab and the total healing. Only God can give the total healing, but we must first go through the healing process and not run from it. Are you ready to be healed of the years of pain that has caused your masks to crumble and fall? God is ready for you to call to Him and say, "Father I have used many substitutes for my pain and I need you now- Help me." Your prayer reaches His heart and He is ready to restore you and lead you to the discovery of who you are divinely called to be.

As we walk this journey of healing together, I want you to know that I understand where you are, because I have been there. I am asking, "Why are you the way you are?" Your walk is my walk. Your struggle is my struggle. You are my daughter, my sister, my friend and I am the one who sees you today, hears you and holds your hand in this journey. My healing does not blind me to the pain of my sisters. In fact, it opens my eyes to those around me needing someone to lift them. I Am You and You are me.

What are you Feeling?

_____

_____

_____

_____

_____

_____

_____

_____

_____

CHAPTER 7

The Search

> *"You will seek Me and find Me when you search for Me with all your heart"*
> (Jeremiah 29:13).

We must understand that in order to give birth to our destiny there will be labor pains of adversity. When I began my search for who I am, I didn't realize it would be more pain and confusion. I was many years beyond my call to God and on the other side of a long marriage. When did I get to this point? How did I get here? Not realizing what I was searching for made life uncomfortable and painful. Everything was turned upside down within me once again as it had been so many years before. This time seemed different. It seemed different because I knew I wasn't alone. I had the assurance that God was with me with each painful step. God is always with us but when we are down so low, our heart, mind and soul feels alone. This time the chaos within me felt like I was in a low state, but I was moving forward for the first time in a long time. I felt hopeful.

Ending a marriage is never easy. I remember just wanting to understand what was happening to me. I felt better about myself, but I was still not sure about many things. Towards the end of my marriage, it didn't seem to provide the false comfort for me that it had for so many years. The pain of change and the uncertainty felt like I was standing back looking at someone else's life and wondering what would happen next. In order for one to find oneself and discover who she is, skeletons are dug up, scabs are no longer gently removed, and he or she is exposed to the pain beneath. Situations, people and the life around us can transform us into who we thought we should be and not necessarily who we really are. Life can bury our true self beneath it. We sometimes live life doing whatever we have to in order to survive the day to day grind.

Discovering the true authentic person underneath my masks required a willingness to trust God and not fight the current of change happening in my life. The strange part about the entire process is I didn't realize I was searching for my true identity. I only knew I felt emotionally stronger than ever before. God desires that we all know who we really are. To know oneself, the process begins with knowing God. He created us. He has seen all the pain we have endured and the protective measures we used to bandage our wounds.

A broken heart can be masked with unforgiveness and bitterness. A heart abused by words of love accompanied by actions that break trust and bring betrayal can be covered with a false sense of boldness that is actually pain. In order to find me underneath all this baggage, I would have to endure the pain covered by my shields. We become vulnerable when we begin the journey of self-discovery. The change that took place inside me when I decided to divorce was that I began to love myself. The clarity of that was not revealed for a while after that decision. I needed to be free for myself. I had always put everyone else's needs and wellbeing before mine in the hopes that someone would do the same for me. Yet, even when we make decisions to better our lives, we must acknowledge that each decision affects not only us but those attached to us. The decision to walk away from my marriage was not only hard and painful for me, but my children were affected. I took what they knew as the norm and family and gave them a new normal, one where their parents were no longer as one. Many asked me, "What about the kids, you have to think about how this will affect them?" Hmm, that's a strange question, right? This question came from those close to me, who meant well, but it upset me. Who else was going to think about the pain my decision would bring upon my children, but me? Yes, I thought of my children and how their world would be shaken. I came to a place where I had to understand what I had shown them was a false sense of love and marriage. I had shown them how you ignore what you want and take what you can get and suffer for years. I had shown them how not to love yourself and wait for others to show you that you are enough. Well, I had to come to the truth that this was not God's best for them. To continue to live a life of existing and not loving myself was no longer going to be my example to them. I told myself I stayed for years because I wanted a family. Yes, that was part of it. The biggest part is I simply wanted to be loved, appreciated and have a family. What are we willing to endure to have love, acceptance and feel worthy? Sometimes we give our hearts over to those who become a Band-Aid to our wounds in the physical in the hope they will heal the wound beneath. I no longer wanted marriage to be my Band-Aid. I wanted and needed to show myself a new and true life filled with love. In doing so, I could help to reestablish this truth for my children. Our children should not be used as an excuse to remain where we are tolerated and not loved. Many times, we can say, "I want my children to have what I didn't have." Until we face the truth of what we have endured and the pain it caused, we will only give them what we know and they deserve so much more. I had carried each of babies within my womb and now it was time to give birth to me, my true self. It was time to birth the woman God created and not the one life created.

Everyone will not understand the process when someone chooses to find out who they really are and live life accordingly. That's okay, live anyway. The power of being healed from years of pain is far greater than concerning ourselves with someone else's opinion. Isn't living according to someone else's plan for us one of the reasons we had to start putting on masks to survive in the first place? In all our lives we must come to a position of, "It's my life and I'm going to live it in my own happiness." It is a position of survival. It demands us to stop searching for happiness and meaning in others. It requires us to stop the rollercoaster of this life we have lived and say, "I am here, I am me and I want to know what makes me who I am."

God created us with a purpose in mind. We are not here by chance or mistake no matter the circumstances surrounding our human conception. When we reach the place in our story where we no longer want to run from self, but to self, then we are in the position to know our purpose and what we are truly meant to do. Most importantly we are ready to discover ourselves, the unique and amazing person that we really are. The search for me was something I never thought would be important. Everyone around me had molded me, with my permission, into who they assumed I needed to be. I gave my permission each time I accepted their treatment as ok, based on what I needed from them. I gave my permission each time I accepted their lies and/or mistreatment and the excuses they gave, as being enough. When searching for love and acceptance outside of God it will always lead to disappointment and frustration. Searching for a greater understanding of who a person is at the center of their being requires one to dig deep within. It requires that we not look for our identity {the name or essential character that identifies somebody or something} in the opinion of others. Search, according to the dictionary, means to discover something by examination; to discover, come to know, or find something by examination.

Examination of the person looking back at you in the mirror can certainly be a type of horror flick that even the title scares you to pieces. To say fear was all inside me is an understatement. Nevertheless, *I felt in my heart that God was with me* and I could do this. Since the word search means to come to know, there must be something about SELF that I don't know. I ran from myself for so long trying to know myself through others. How amazing it is to know that in order to BE who we are, we have to come back to ourselves. The very person we have run from for so long, is the very person we have to uncover and discover in order to know who we are. When you think about running away from yourself, what does this look like? Well, it looks like you making a decision, as I did, to do whatever you had to and become whomever you needed to become in order to stop the pain and put a band-aide over it. The more you do this, the less you can identify when you are hurting. We can become a chameleon in our life. I remember when God showed me that is who I was. A chameleon can change their colors based on their surroundings as a way to hide themselves from a threat. It is a way of protection. God showed me it is also manipulation. Yes, manipulation. Let's just call it what it is, because this keeps us in an authentic place, right? We run from what we don't want to feel. We change our personality, words, clothes, morals, and become what our surroundings will accept or deem worthy. Ouch, did I step on your toes? I hope so, because I want your eyes wide open so you can be free. It made me say ouch when God said I was a chameleon. It hurt deeply, or should I say felt embarrassed, when He showed me it was manipulation. To me this meant that I was manipulating just like those I gave permission to in my life that inflicted pain. They were manipulating me. We were manipulating each other. Go figure. Can we say Ouch again? The journey to self is one where over and over again we must accept the truth in the mirror as our truth. We must accept how this makes us feel. These are the steps needed to take off the chameleon character and change our attire. It is a rebirth. It is an examination. It is a discovery. It is the best journey you will ever embark upon.

That person is ME! Yes, it is ME! The person who always felt she didn't fit in with anyone. I am the person looking for a man to give her the love her father didn't. I am the person looking to feel wanted. I am the person who became who she had to be in order to get attention. I became who I thought I should be because I did not feel the real me was worth anything. Yes, that was me. I had to look at myself. I needed to look at my wounds, my broken heart, my disappointments, my mistakes. My lack of worth and value needed to be examined. All that I had become needed to be examined to find out who I truly was for the first time in my life. I must to be ready because God had brought me to this place and He knew I was ready even if I didn't think so. My search brought me face to face with someone I had not known for forty plus years, *ME*. The search required digging, scraping and surgery of my heart and soul. There could not be excuses or denials during the search because it would hinder where I was going. The search was no longer an option but a necessity.

Are you ready? I believe you are reading these words right now because you are ready to look at the very things you have run from all your life. You are ready to turn back to the mirror, look into the eyes staring back at you and say, "This is Me, I am here and I will no longer turn away." God has brought you here to go on your journey, one step at a time. Your search is for now. You have everything within you to examine and uncover who you really are. You can remove the character of a chameleon and begin to peel back the layers of lies and embrace truth. Are you ready? God knows you are or you would have turned away by now or retreated. This time your healing is no longer an option but a necessity. Hand in hand we will walk through this process together. Let's Go.

What are you Feeling?

_____

_____

_____

_____

_____

_____

_____

_____

CHAPTER 8

The Process

"...He who began a good work in you will perfect it until the day of Christ Jesus"
(Philippians 1:6).

Process in the dictionary is defined as, the action of going forward {Dictionary.com}. This was definitely where I was, right dab in the middle of going forward. Going forward requires that you have to look back, evaluate and explore what is behind that brought you into this moment. Process is just that, a process. It is a movement. Process is constant and not always steady. Moving forward is necessary in all our lives to not become stagnant. For many of us, looking backwards into our past brings about self-judgment and despair that can halt us in place. We can become stuck in the moment of pain and abuse and not be able to see any possibility of moving forward. Today we are doing this a little different. We are going to give ourselves permission to go forward by allowing ourselves the grace to face one part of our journey and deal with it. Only one thing at a time. For me, I could go down memory lane and only see pain, denial, promiscuity, stupid choices, fear and so much more. The thoughts would overwhelm and eventually bind my hands, mind and feet. The process of self-discovery this time was different because I knew God was guiding me and not me rushing down the road of my past all alone. When we know and accept this, we can exhale and take another step in this new process of healing.

I've said many times before that looking at yourself and discovering who you are requires courage. Courage means the quality of mind or spirit that enables a person to face difficulty, danger or pain without showing fear {Dictionary.com}. I can't say that my process has been without fear but my spirit felt strong enough to move with the plan set before me. I felt that I had been living fearful all my life and even if it was a morsel of courage, I felt it.

In looking back at my marriage, I realized that I married for many reasons. Two of the main reasons were my lack of confidence that anyone would love me and my lack of self-worth. It was not my ex-husbands fault that I chose to accept what he gave me as enough. I married out of desperation. Did I love him? Yes, I loved him, but we were not in love at that time. Although I believed what I felt for him was true love. The reasons for getting married varies from one person to another. I believed that I had found true love but, in reality, I now understand that I married at the point of my pain and self-esteem. I didn't have any self-esteem. I felt I had finally found someone who chose me over the other women and I dived in head first. At the time I didn't know what love was, but this was as good as any. There is not any blame towards my ex-husband for my choice to get married. I have come to a place in my heart where I accept where I was in life at that time. This is what I knew of love.

My life for twenty years produced five beautiful children, one who is in heaven. I'm glad I married the man who gave me a new name and with whom God allowed me to conceive these blessings of little ones. My babies were worth saying I do. My children's father was and is a part of the process of my self-discovery. Every part of my life God is using to bring me to this place in my story. There was a time when looking back at my reasons for getting married and staying married brought frustration and anger. I now know that in order to move along in the process I had to own my responsibility in my choice. Ownership of our choices is a power move in the process of healing. It is a hard thing to do, but a necessary decision. Facing our truth is healing. Denying it leaves us in a place I call, Victim Hood. I had a T-shirt and billboard for my Hood. Victim Hood is a place where everyone else is to blame for who we are, the decisions we made and why we cannot heal. We become the CEO, president and neighborhood representative. What hood are you repping? As you follow the process to overcome the wounds within your soul, you have to give yourself permission to no longer allow Victim Hood to be place of residence. Yes, it is easier to blame others, no matter the responsibility they have, than to face ourselves in the mirror. Because God has you here reading these words, I believe that just like me, it is time for your eviction notice from Victim Hood. You have the choice to stay there or leave. So, I ask you how has the old neighborhood served you so far? Not to good, right? In that case, shift into the possibilities of living in a place of wholeness instead of being a victim to what you have endured.

Low self-esteem is a wound. Having a low self-image or belief of oneself- is not being humble, it is being without the knowledge of Self Worth and Self Value. Low self-esteem is a burden on the heart and spirit of a person. It is a burden because you have this image of yourself as being less than the next person and not feeling worthy to be loved or wanted. The weight of believing you are less than someone else comes from not knowing who you are. Allowing your life experiences to tell you that no matter what you do or who you become, you will never measure up, is also a heavy weight to carry. Low self-esteem is a wound that produces that weight. God will teach us how to use this weight for our good and not against us as we go through the process of healing. As we acknowledge self-esteem we shine light on it. Shining light on anything takes away its power to hide and deceive. Once its' hiding place is visible, the strength and weight it had over us, lessens. This is how it works for our good. We use the weight of it and begin to lift it off of us, therefore increasing our muscles of self-worth and self-love. It is a wound that can only begin to heal as you choose to believe and accept

God's unconditional love for you. It is my belief that the root of low self-esteem is not feeling loved. Family members, lovers and friends may tell you that they love you, but when their actions don't prove it, you are left feeling unloved. No one has had a "perfect" upbringing. Some of us have gone through some of the same things and yet they have affected our lives differently. I didn't receive the love needed as a child and that affected me in many ways. I hungered for it and sometimes, unknowingly, withheld it from my children and those close to me. We all deal with our wounds differently. I wanted love at any cost to me. However, I did not know that I was selling myself the short end of the stick in my search.

The cost of my self-esteem and self-worth was too high of a price to pay. I paid with my body, my mind, my heart, my self-esteem, my self-worth, my morals, my mind and it was still not enough to receive what I needed. I lost so much fighting for love. I gave all of me and received not much in return. Was it worth the cost? Of course not, but when you are hungry, you eat. I was hungry for love and acceptance and I used what I had to buy it. In the end I lost me and all the value that came with me. I gave freely of myself and saw my dignity fall into the dirt. Our self-esteem is shattered when we search for what we need to feel whole in others. The process to move forward requires us to again, be honest with ourselves with where we are, how we got here, and taking ownership of our part in our story. The process of finding the healing of low self-esteem begins in accepting first that we are low in confidence, we have a shortage of love for ourselves and we are hungry to be loved.

My process began with a thought to move forward. It begins in the heart that desires to heal. It begins in being tired of feeling broken. My process started before I said, "I want a divorce." Inside my mind and soul, I knew something had changed in my norm and I was changing. It was confusing to me. It was a twinkle of strength that propelled me into the unknown. I realized that I didn't have to search for daddy's love anymore. The pure joy of realizing my birth father loved me in his way and the way he knew to love me, had begun the healing in my heart. I searched in men to find that love, but I was coming into the truth that this type of search brought me to a place of pain. Now my Heavenly Father was taking me to a new place. Even though God reveals to us the root of our issues, it is still up to us to let go or hold on. Sometimes we hold on to pain and anger because we tell ourselves we are not going to let the people off the hook who hurt us. In all honesty by holding on to the pain, we deepen the grip their acts have on us and deepen the wounds we try and hide. It is a gift to ourselves when we allow the process of healing to move us from victim to overcomer by letting go.

As I write this, God gave me a vision of steps leading up to a light. At the bottom of the steps were shadows and darkness but I can see the light brightly shining at the top of the stairs. The first step to the process begins in a dark place. The dark place inside us that has been covered in shame, pain, heartache, disappointment and sadness has seemed too sore to be touched. As the process of healing begins, this same dark place now sees a flicker of light and the darkness is drawn to it. There is something within us that recognizes the light drawing us out of the dark place as hope and we can take a step towards it. Starting at the base of the stairs looking at how far you have to go is scary. Looking upward and wondering if you have the strength to take each step makes your head spin. Taking the first step upward out of the pit of your soul and mind is the most earth shattering step you can take. Imagine the step of a giant upon the earth and it begins to crumble because of the strength of the excessively large person. When we take that first step towards our process of discovery, the ground inside us where our heart and soul dwell is shaken. There is a shaking because the power of God is shaking things up within. I'm amazed how when we least expect it, God reaches out his hand and shows us it is time to move and go forward. Everything in your life denies that truth and looks like you will never move out of the concrete around your feet and heart. Yet God reaches through all the weeds and masks and says, "Come!" The process has begun. You are on your way. Don't stop now. You found the courage to move this far so don't give up now. There is a stirring in your soul that you've never known and God says, "Come to me and I will walk with you into the light." Are you ready to begin? Well I can say from experience that if you were not ready, God would not have allowed you to reach this point. Knowing this should give you the assurance that He is with you and the best is yet to come. There will be tears as you reflect, inspect and do inventory. Do not fret, for it is for your good. You are on the road to self-discovery and healing. As you begin to feel the earthquake within you and everything you knew in your mind is moving from its' position, do not fear for God's hand is at work. He has allowed the wheat and the tares to grow within and now He is separating them. Take another step and know It is well.

What are you Feeling?

CHAPTER 9

Climb Up

"But the God of all grace, who hath called us unto his eternal glory by Christ Jesus, after that ye have suffered a while, make you perfect, stablish, strengthen, settle you. To him be glory and dominion for ever and ever"
(I Peter 5:10-11).

We have talked about taking a step forward in order to go through the process required to get from where you are to the place where healing is possible for you. Each person's journey to finding themselves is different. In the next few chapters I want to share with you some of the steps that I've taken to find out who I am with God's help. It is a process of steps to reach any destination of change. This is our life so these are not steps to completion but steps of healing. As I stated in the last chapter, process is the action of moving forward. When you don't know where you are going, it is hard to just move forward. God will guide us through every step of finding ourselves if we can trust Him.

In the last chapter I mentioned the vision God gave me of being at the bottom of a dark stairwell but seeing light at the top. This is how my journey of starting to find out who I am began. It looked very dark within me because the place I was in was unfamiliar and scary. As I think back to those dark stairs I knew that I had changed. I felt love for myself and that made me uncomfortable. I felt strong and weak at the same time. I wanted to go forward but did not know how. I felt a pull in my spirit, and I knew that God was with me even though He was audibly quiet. Steps lead us up or down. Steps can be tall or low, but they serve the same purpose and that is to take us from one place to another. Our life choices and circumstances have been steps to bring us to this moment. In this moment you get to decide your next step. Yes, you choose. Life and other people have chosen our next step for us as they fed upon our wounds like vultures. They could recognize our raw places because they had the same raw places within them. They maneuvered us into the plan they had for us and knew how hungry we were for love and acceptance. We took a step with them that led us to more pain. We took steps downward when we saw love running away. We took a step upward when someone or some-thing came along looking like a shiny new penny. We chased it down in our mind and our actions. However, remember as we are looking back and evaluating where we were and where we are, we are no longer reppin our old stomping ground,

Victim Hood. We are taking ownership of what we find on our examination and dealing with it.

It is time for God's children to rediscover who He created us to be. The world has caused us to put on so many masks that we don't know who we are. The dark places inside us have crushed our spirit and soul and pushed us to search outside ourselves in hopes of knowing who we are.

My road is different from yours but our wounds recognize each other. The same way our wounds recognize each other in relationships in the name of love, is the same way when we are ready to heal. We recognize when our sister is wounded in the same place. Even if we are one step ahead of her, it gives a space of clarity that allows us to now see our sister on the step below us and help to pull her up. By me sharing my journey with you, I am able to reach you and pull you up because now I have clarity. The steps don't make us more than or less than those around us. It simply shows us what is possible and where we don't want to go back to. It's that simple. Sometimes we find ourselves on the step in between and we can fall back on our old way of thinking and begin to compare ourselves. STOP! When you are going through the process and those old ways rise up and they will, call on God again with the simple prayer, "God Help Me."

What steps are we courageous enough to take to find our authentic self? If we knew everything that we would need to dig up, recognize and own about ourselves it can make the upward stair climb terrifying. Coming to a place of being tired of filling empty inside, confused and wondering where we stand in this huge world is the perfect place to be. Why, you may ask? It is because when we come to that place we have come to the end of self and are ready for change from what we have considered the normal and desire wholeness. No longer does the makeup, the titles, the men, the shopping, the money, the drugs, the alcohol serve as numbing agents for our pain. No longer are we wanting to make excuses for where we have come in our lives, but we desire to be free from the darkness within. The end of the masks that we have worn to cover our fragile self-confidence no longer cover us. God has ordered our steps {Psalms 37:23} and now it is time to begin our journey into self-discovery.

It is an amazing journey and you have found the courage to begin the climb up the stairs to your destiny. You have chosen to move upward in faith because you have realized you are more than you have believed. Your struggles in life brought you to this point in your story and God is not surprised. You may not realize it right now, as I didn't in the beginning, that you have found strength hidden within you that you never knew you had. Your story has turned the page and a new chapter has begun. Choosing to begin again is brave. The unknown is on each step on the climb upward. The first step is the biggest, but your legs have been strengthened for the climb. Your legs maybe a little shaky but God will hold you steady.

If we have lived through the pain of our past, we can certainly live through this journey. We are about to unveil the real person behind the eyes that look back at us in the mirror. Who is she, Really? What secrets does she hold in her heart? What pain has she buried within her soul that she has pretended didn't exist? The eyes that have looked back at you for years are finding new life and soon they will sparkle with the love you have missed out on for so long. You have not really looked at your eyes because it has been too painful. Instead you chose to fix your hair, wear the right makeup thinking that would brighten you.

What we have done for far too long is pretend. We became comfortable with pretending because it was easier than dealing with who we had become. This takes us back to the chameleon spirit. Pretending is manipulation. It is giving ourselves in a dishonest way. Take responsibility and free yourself. This is how we learned to face life. We have been in survival mode and walking as zombies being led by the wounds of others connecting with our wounds. God has been with you always. Now, you recognize He is with you because with each step you take forward and upward you become clearer and more aware that you are not alone. What we know, we are accountable for. Before we knew, it was easy to be naive and be ok with what we do. Do not beat yourself up for your life skills that got you to this point but be grateful that God is with you on this new journey as He was all through your life. Your cry for help has been answered and change has begun. You didn't arrive at this point in your story by chance. All your prayers and all your tears have been heard and now it is time to take another step. Take a deep breath, exhale and move forward towards finding yourself. Turn the page in your story because a new manuscript is starting and you are the main character.

What are you Feeling?

PART 2

INTERLUDE

Here we are. We have dealt with our current state of existence. We have discovered that God's love is the love we have always needed in order to feel wanted, loved and accepted. We have learned to face the woman in the mirror and not run away from her. Running away from who we see in the mirror is partially why we don't know who we are at our core.

We took a step and found that one sister is a step ahead and one is behind us. What about the sister who is on the same step as you? We forgot about her. She is climbing through her journey and you both have arrived at the same step. Both of you are on this journey of self-discovery. The journey where you have tried so many times and each time you saw someone ahead of you, you became intimidated. You allowed yourself to shrink down because you felt you weren't good enough. Now you see that there is another sister standing beside you. You look at her and she seems to be very familiar to you, yet you cannot remember where you know her from. Look a little deeper. Draw closer to her. Step into her space and look her in the eyes.

As a smile warms your face, you realize it is the reflection of the rebellious child within you. The one who was abused, raped, molested, abandoned, made to feel unwanted and unloved, who lost her voice, she is walking with you. For so long, she, your inner child was rebellious and acted out of the pain still dwelling within you. Each time someone said they loved you and they would stay with you, she rebelled and reminded you of the many times you were told that and still, they left.

Yet, through your journey and resilience you both are here together. No longer separated but becoming one. You see, those around you can see a woman of a certain age. They see her bold, outspoken, career driven and sometimes sad. What we have needed is for someone to not only see our brightness but to look a little deeper and ask, "Why are you sad?" They have tried to engage the adult woman, not realizing the woman they saw was a broken little girl who lost her sass, as she lost her voice. She lost her spunk the first time she was sexually abused. She lost her ability to speak up or use her NO in a powerful way. Yet, today, through God's love she is growing up into the woman you are today.

At every level of our journey, God goes into the deepest corners of our soul and finds the broken and shattered pieces of who we were and brings us into unison with ourselves. You have been shattered in so many pieces, there is no way you could know your true identity.

So, reach over to the immature part of you standing on the steps as you look up to the light above and take the next step together. Soon, through God's grace, mercy, love and acceptance you will no longer have to look to the side to see your growth, healing, strength and joy. It will overflow as a well from within you.

It is time to follow the steps to your healing. Each Step is part of the process to answer the question that has been replaying in your mind, "Who Am I, Really?

In the chapters to follow, I will share with you some of the steps God allowed me to take to reach the light I saw in the vision He gave me. Remember, the start of the process begins in darkness. There will be days and nights where you will find yourself feeling as if you are not moving forward or you have been on the same step too long. Trust the process and do not give up. You have come too far to go back now. As you walk this journey, don't forget your sister behind you. She is watching you and waiting for you to go forward so she has an example of what is possible for her. For now, focus on you and allow God to lead.

This is your moment and the light is drawing you. Let's go forward.

CHAPTER *10*

Step 1: Climb The Stairs-In Fear

"Have I not commanded you? Be strong and courageous...for the LORD your God will be with you wherever you go"
(Joshua 1:9).

Y ou are on your way already with this step because you have realized the real you is hidden under your pain and fears and you want more for your life. You are fearful because you don't know what you will go through but you keep moving. I was in a marriage that I realized I no longer wanted to be in. I felt empty and lost. I was angry. I wasn't sure if I was angry at my husband, myself or the unknown feelings going on inside me. The feeling of fear overwhelmed me. I questioned all the emotions I felt. The pain in my soul seemed fresh. What I discovered was moving forward doesn't always feel brave. Actually, it is the total opposite. I had wanted things to change for me before but I always changed my mind when it became too painful and scary. God gave me the sense that this time I truly could go forward even though I was afraid.

To look at yourself and not know who you are is scary. To not know what love is, is one thing, but to not know how to love yourself is painful. Fear is paralyzing and it can be one reason why we choose to live the lie we know as life. The desire to know who you are deep within must outweigh the fear of taking a step towards your future. Fear told me that it was too much to want to change, but my spirit was pushing me forward. The face and eyes looking back at me in the mirror were unfamiliar. They were unfamiliar because normally I looked at my face and hair to fix it but now I had to see me. My desire to see the truth about me was lifting my eyes. The brown eyes that I ran from were drawing me to seek them and what was behind them. My eyes held secrets to my soul and identity. Life struggles had boxed me into an angry, bitter, insecure and broken woman who now was alone. Marriage didn't fix me nor did having children. After all this time my inner being was screaming to me, "You are greater than you have believed." Could I possibly be more than I had believed all my life? Could I be more than the person who believed she was not wanted or loved by anyone? The answer to those questions was now, yes.

God was beginning a new chapter in my story. I was at place in life where fear hadn't left but it was now facing faith. I wanted to be free in every sense of the word. My heart was hungry for love and to be loved. As I remember listening to the John Legend song, "All of Me," I recalled how I felt Gods' love for me for the first time. Love was calling me out of my dungeon. Love was holding my hand and guiding me forward. Trauma brings fear. I had faced much trauma in my life, and I wanted to know triumph.

Fear is an illusion that the devil uses to bind us where we are in life. Faith is the truth that God is in control and He has everything under control. Even in fear declare to yourself that the God who is in control is in control of each step forward and fear will have to die off. God created us for greatness. The things that have happened in our lives were to bring fear as we become older and keep us from our destiny. Those same things were to rob us of our identity. We were made to feel that who we were was not enough to be loved, to be treated with respect or to not be abused. God is restoring our identity and we shall find our true identity in Him. His love for us never changed. His purpose for our lives never changed. When we become strong enough to say, enough is enough, then we are ready to allow His grace and mercy to walk us through the journey.

To know who you are requires one to dig up old wounds. The wounds in our soul need to heal so we can move out of the cycle that we have lived in. The cage door to our soul has been sprung open by God. We no longer have to crouch down in the corners of life and watch everyone else live. We can discover who is hidden within the person staring back in the mirror. We are unique. In order for us to grow, we must embrace who we were, accept who are in this moment and accept who we are purposed to be.

Our laughter is not like any other. I learned along the way that I like my laugh. I had hidden my laugh for so long because I thought it was loud. The more I would hear my belly laughter, the more I loved it. I discovered that I liked being silly with my kids when I had always been so serious. I remember praying to God, "Give me my childlike laughter back" and He did just that. The more I laughed, the more I smiled. Fear had stolen my smile and my laughter and with God answering my call for help, it had been rebirthed within me. I thought if others heard my laugh it would provide one more reason for them to judge me as being not good enough. Fear comes in many forms but the root of it all is deception. If our minds can remain in fear and doubt we can stay paralyzed. Yet the moment we decide within our heart that we are ready to break free, God is there with open arms. Fear has had the keys to the doors in front of us with guards of deception, trauma, shame and hopelessness. As we see the stairs before us, they seem insurmountable, which means incapable of being overcome {Dictionary.com}. Each time we raise our foot to take the first step, then another, the stairs seem to move away. In times past, I would allow the stairs to move and I would walk away. I realize now it was because I did not believe I could be any better than before. As God showed me the vision of the darkness turning to light, it began to look possible. So, with fear beating down on me and a twinkle of hope, I took the first step. You can too. I am as you are. You are as I am. Take the steps even in fear toward the light before you. Your life shall never be the same. Go forth towards your destiny and watch fear disappear and lose its power in your life. The little bird is becoming an Eagle and can soar high above the cares of life. It's your time to fly.

What are you Feeling?

CHAPTER 11

Step Two: Acknowledge Your Pain, Willingly

> *"He heals the brokenhearted and binds up their wounds"* (Psalm 147:3).

The masks we wear or have worn to get us through the day have been to cover us so no one would know we are broken in mind, spirit and heart. It is time to be honest with ourselves and admit that we have been hurt and we are hurting. Continuing to push down your emotions about abuse, being rejected by those who are to protect you, and abandoned by those that said they loved you keeps you buried at the point of the pain. Shine light in the darkness and make the secrets known if only to you. One has to face where they are in the moment to heal. Pain is deafening. Abandonment makes us hold to people that we should release but we hold on with desperation so we won't feel that feeling of being abandoned again. We can't heal what we are not willing to face. Are you angry? Are you depressed? Are you bitter? Whatever your questions are there is a root to them. Anger, depression, fear, rage, bitterness are the results of hurt and pain. You deserve to be free from it all. Yes, you deserve to be free no matter what has happened. You can come across as angry and bitter and yet your eyes speak of a sadness that goes so deep. It is so deep that you can't see past it or dare to feel anything other than the pain. To allow yourself to feel gives light where only darkness has lived.

God allowed some amazing women to come into my life many years ago. One of them was named Louise. I spoke of her earlier. She was such a loving and strong woman. Another was named Carolyn. These women were my spiritual mothers. They may never know the impact they would have in my life so many years later. The ministry that they led allowed women to find their identity in Christ Jesus and love themselves through Christ's love for them. Carolyn had a part of the ministry where we would take a mirror and hold it up to our eyes and speak affirmations to ourselves based on scripture. When I first started doing this, I would look in the mirror and find nothing but fault with what I saw. She would say, "Stop picking at her and look in her eyes." She was speaking of the person staring back at me in the mirror. Years later, I would have to stop picking at her (myself) again and look into my eyes to deal with who I was and who I had become.

God brings people into our lives to plant seeds of thoughts, words and ideas. Many years later those seeds are giving life to my soul. We look in the mirror and we see all our flaws. Do we ever say, "I'm like this because I was sexually abused and I hate myself?" Do we say, "I am this way because I was abandoned?" Do we admit that we have to be stern so no one hurts or rejects us again? Do we admit that because we were rejected we won't allow anyone to get close out of fear of being rejected again? Do we simply own our truth? No, we probably do not because we haven't had the courage to do so. We believe the cycle will continue and tear our already fragile heart apart. We just walk around clothed in shame and anger because it is all we know. We no longer have to "pick at her" and only see faults but now we can be delivered.

The root of pain is where the answers to all the questions are about why we are who we are and why we respond to life the way we do. Getting to the root and pulling it up will open the wound and bring us out of hiding. I had to deal with the fact that I had felt abandoned all my life. My truth is that I felt I was alone and unloved. My truth is I was rejected and felt unwanted. Being molested by family members intensified feelings of being unprotected and unloved. When trying to tell my mom about this when I became an adult, it was brushed aside. I had buried all my pain under manipulation, desperation, inferiority, insecurity, insignificance, anger and sadness. I needed to breathe and discovering that I wasn't mentally ill only spiritually broken, was allowing me to do just that. God was strengthening my spirit and I felt free for the first time in years. I was beginning to look in the mirror and see my eyes and learning to love what I saw. My eyes would have a twinkle sometimes and when more pain would come to memory, the twinkle would fade away. However; the memory of the joy I felt when I could be honest with what I felt and why, was outweighing my need to remain in sadness.

A caged bird can sing, but a bird without boundaries can soar. I could see myself beginning to soar. Here I was on the other side of a twenty-year marriage and beginning to find myself. I determined that what I found wasn't so bad. Acknowledging my pain and where I was in life was bringing fear, but it was also giving me life. Working through any trauma is hard, but know it is better to live in the joy of breakthrough than to die in the pain of despair. I had given myself permission to live and live is exactly what God purposed for me to do {John 10:10}. Living life with new oxygen in your lungs is a sign that you are breathing in as God gives you His breath. When you are stuck in the pain your lungs, your soul and your heart feel like you are being suffocated from the inside out. Acknowledging the pain opens us up to fresh air that expands our hidden places so we can catch our breath and live. It is life acknowledging there is more to do and you must breathe in order to do so.

What are you Feeling?

_____

_____

_____

_____

_____

_____

_____

_____

_____

_____

CHAPTER 12

Step 3: Face The Pain

*"Just as I am, without one plea, but that thy blood
was shed for me, and that thou bid'st me come to
thee, O Lamb of God, I come. I come"*
("Just As I Am" by Charlotte Elliott, 1835).

Now that we have acknowledged our inner pain we must choose to deal with it and not deny it to ourselves any longer. When we deal with it we are facing it. We are facing fear head on and saying, "No More." The masks were to cover the wounds from the pain. The masks begin to crack when we acknowledge the pain. They begin to fall when we face it. We have lived life wounded this far because we have tried to run away from that which caused our soul to ball into the fetal position. In order to discover who we are behind the mask, one has to find a morsel of strength, take a deep breath and face the open wounds of their soul.

My heart longed to be loved, protected, appreciated and wanted. My attitude, my personality, my anger, my up and down ways were the result of being needy of love. I used anger as my defense so no one would hurt me, yet I desperately wanted them to like me. I felt if I came across as a raging bull in my attitude and words, then I wouldn't be bullied as I was as a child. I didn't realize I was rebelling every good thing I wanted and needed with the anger, but it was all I knew to do. Searching for love in other people is what I had come to know as normal. As God began to open up my heart, I realized His Love for me covers all the hurt from not being loved. The anger came from frustration of having to be in control of me for so long. I felt no one else would protect me because they hadn't before. I was literally mentally and emotionally exhausted from feeling I had to do whatever was necessary to protect myself from others. I felt there was no one who gave me a safe place to lay my head as an escape from the torment I felt inside. There were many days I felt like a refugee having no place to call safe and always on the run in my mind and emotions.

In order to move forward, the past must be faced. There is no other way to do it. Facing all those wounds inside me would be painful, but I didn't want those wounds to give me the false sense of protection anymore. I saw a woman in the mirror but God was showing me the broken little girl within. The soul never forgets the pain and wants us to act out of them. The soul must submit to The Word of God if we are to see ourselves for who we are. The carnal (flesh) part of us has to submit to The Spirit of God in order to see our truth.

Facing the fact that you were sexually abused as a child or an adult means you may have to relive those moments and face your feelings of someone else being in control and taking your innocence. Reliving the truth that three of my cousins molested me and seeing their faces in my spirit was traumatizing. The questions of why they would do that to me repeated in my head. The men who were friends of the family told me I was beautiful and touched me when they felt the desire to do so. The hardest part was accepting that I loved the attention. A part of me knew it was wrong, but the part of me that craved love and attention drew from it like a well that contained my last drink of water. Here I was years later feeling distraught because my need to be noticed and my desperation for love had caused me to receive it in any way possible. Those thoughts made me weep. I could feel the pain so deep it was almost unbearable. Thinking about this caused shame to swell up within me and overflow. As I gave myself permission to feel what those thoughts brought with them, shame did not want to release me.

There was no one to talk to about what was happening to me as a child and I felt alone. This made me feel unwanted and abandoned. Where were the people who said they loved me and who were supposed to protect me? Did they not see that something was wrong with me? Many years later tears poured from me not as a woman but as a broken child. Our journey to facing what has happened to us may be the last thing we want to do but it is a necessary battle to live your life being who you were purposed to be. God already knows how deep the wounds go and He knows what we have been trying to cover up just so we can live life daily. His best for His children is that we break the hold that pain, shame, hatred, unforgiveness, doubt and bitterness have in our lives.

The desire to be real with yourself and to own your truth has brought you here. You are in a position to be free from the past demons that haunt you today. You are giving birth to the real you hidden underneath the brokenness, the anger and the fear. You no longer have to be crouched down waiting for the knight on the white horse to come save you. God is here for you as He is for me. He rescued me from me, and He will do the same for you. Facing your truth will cause some dark days and nights, but it will not compare to the new life waiting for you beyond it. Face your pain knowing that you are not alone in doing so. What the abusers stole from you, God will restore {Psalms 51:12}. Each day becomes better when we walk with Jesus instead of trying to be our own protector. A child needs a brave soldier to go before them and destroy the enemies as they approach. God is brave enough for you. You are Gods' daughter. He is destroying the enemies of your soul that have been your shield, your comfort and tormentors within. The battle is won. Your steps to self-discovery are powerful ones. You are on your way into greatness and all you have needed is being provided. Receive it. It is that simple. Receiving something is to accept it. No more hiding in the shadows. Choosing to face the scary monster that represents the past shows faith. Thinking back as a child, when watching scary movies, we are afraid to turn off the lights in fear that the monster in the movie would be under our bed. As we wrap ourselves up in pain and shame of the past, those wounds become our monsters. Every time we tried to live beyond the boundaries of those wounds, the monster would rise up like a wall and stop us in our tracks. As you find courage to no longer coward down to the monsters and stand up to them, you are gaining an inner boldness and courage you never believed you would ever have. By doing this we have taken another step up the stairs toward the brightness. The knight on the white horse is the illusion of a savior. Jesus is the Savior. You have lived with illusions of love, peace, comfort, protection for far too long. No one can rescue and restore us the way He can and will.

What are you Feeling?

_____

_____

_____

_____

_____

_____

_____

_____

_____

CHAPTER *13*

Step 4: Release The Pain

"Let all bitterness, and wrath, and anger, and clamour...be put away from you"
(Ephesians 4:31).

The root of the pain has been brought to our attention. All the many years of asking and wondering who we are has brought us to this place of getting to the root of the pain. It is not enough to admit we were hurt and acknowledging that there has been pain. The pain must also be released. As God reveals to us our inner wounds they can begin to heal, inside out. No longer can we be in denial of what has happened to us in our lives. Our desire to know who we really has opened up those scabbed over wounds. In order to heal them completely, one of the things that must be done is beginning the process of releasing the pain, one moment at a time. I say one moment at a time because I remember one day I said, "I'm going to make it one day at a time." It seemed as soon as I finished the first word, I felt God saying, "Sometimes the thought of taking a day at a time can be overwhelming, so take one moment at a time." WOW! For many of us, we have held on to the trauma and toxic relationships we have lived through for most, if not all of our lives. To try and go through the process of healing taking big steps, can become overwhelming. Take one moment at a time and walk through this process, don't rush, just move. The release is something you must be willing to do. The same way we were holding on to things (thoughts, ideas, expectations, etc.) is the same way we must be willing to let go of what no longer serves us.

It is not easy to admit that for the majority of your life you were rejected by your father, and you didn't feel loved by him. It's not easy to say to yourself that you needed love so much that you allowed men to treat you with the same disregard and emotional abuse you felt as a child just to feel some sense of love. To see myself in that light was dark for me. Again, the shame rose up within me like the deep red sea. I would feel overcome with emotions and thoughts of how I looked to others, how I felt about myself and if I would ever change. I never wanted to feel the way I did emotionally and mentally while I searched for love in people, especially men. The pain of what I felt I needed to do in order to be loved was bad enough, but I remembered how I felt sickened to my stomach allowing the men and boys to touch and invade my body all in hopes of them rising up and to tell me, "I love you." As I asked God who I was, my past would rear its' head and sometimes it was not easy to continue the self-discovery. My desire to be free from who I knew myself to be, was weighing heavier on my heart than the pain. I began to realize that I needed some understanding as to why these things happened to me.

A wounded woman relates to the father that rejected her as the little girl that felt the sting of abandonment every time. I asked God, "Why did you allow this man to be my dad when you knew he would make me feel this way?" God gave me the understanding that my father and mother gave me what they knew to give me based on what they were given as children and young adults. God revealed that they loved me the way they understood to show love. Even though it left me angry and bitter for most of my life, now I have compassion for my parents. I came to the understanding that I needed a new perspective towards my parents and anyone else that had wounded my soul. I needed to stop relating to my parents as the little girl and start relating to them as the adult I had become with the healing I was gaining. I am still learning to do this even today. When I feel the struggle overtaking me, I have to pray and ask God to help me.

Accepting the truth and walking in it are big steps to take. These ideals of love and affection had framed my whole image of love. My vision was distorted, and I didn't know what love was. To continue to blame our outburst and actions on someone that hurt us gives them power and diminishes our own. I wanted my power back. As I stated before, God began to show me that I no longer needed to search for daddy's love anymore in men. I had found the love I searched for in my Lord and Savior Jesus Christ.

Releasing pain to Jesus is what we must do once the truth of the pain is revealed. It is not always a one-step process. Sometimes it takes more than just a single prayer to God to let go of what has been holding on to us. My prayer to God was that I was laying my pain regarding different situations in my life at His feet. I desired to leave them there and walk away in freedom. Then another thought would come up from the past, and it seemed the pain was fresh again. I felt defeated and didn't think anything would change ever in my life. I came to the understanding that my wounds went deep. When I prayed to leave things at His feet, God answered me but I didn't always release them to Him. The pain had been my normal for so long that to not have it was uncomfortable. No matter how bad I felt, I knew how to operate in pain and as a victim. I knew how this felt and somewhat knew what to expect. The thought of not knowing what would happen as I released my pain to God, was overwhelming. Yet, I understood through my tears that crying out to God while constantly bringing to the surface the pain lying at the surface of everything I did, had to become my new normal. In order to deal with what I carried in my soul for so long, my normal had to be disrupted.

Prayers have to become more honest. Thinking that God doesn't know what we feel and not being honest with Him in prayer only hinders the one praying. Hebrews 4:15 states, "For we have not a high priest which cannot be touched with the feeling of our infirmities." The pain can become so unbearable that the only way to get release is to tell God what you really feel. I can remember crying so hard and asking God, "Why do I hurt so badly and why does it go so deep?" This was the moment my prayers became more personal with God. I never felt I had anyone to really be honest with in my life so no one really knew how deeply I hurt. God was transitioning my life through prayer, my honest prayers without my masks. Psalms 51:17 says, "The sacrifices of God are a broken spirit: a broken and a contrite heart." A contrite heart is caused by or showing sincere remorse. I had prayed through my masks far too long.

When masks are the daily attire we begin to not only see those around us as someone we need to hide ourselves from, but we also see God as someone we have to hide our true self from. God knows the deepness of the pain and the wounds that we have lived out of. He wants us to trust Him enough to remove our masks and come behind the holy veil and be transparent with Him. This is not easy because it requires vulnerability. Vulnerability requires a step of faith._Vulnerability is exposure. So ask yourself is it worth me opening my wounds up to God completely to discover who I really am? Is it worth going out on a limb to trust the one and only One who has loved you before you were conceived? For me the answer is, Yes. I had come to a place in my life where I was tired of running from myself, and I wanted to know myself, so this was my requirement and my option. It was a matter of life and death.

Giving my pain and my actions to God opened more doors for me. I started to see myself as an adult and not a child. I would correct myself at times based on what God was showing me about me. I would laugh at myself sometimes as I spoke out loud that I would no longer act a certain way because I knew better now. Each time God reveals a part of our lives to us that has been horrific, we must choose to release that pain to Him after we acknowledge it and own it as our truth.

Release means to me that I can no longer use my pain as an excuse to be negative. I cannot allow men who aren't good for me into my life, just to feel loved. Releasing also means I am not allowing other people to hurt me because it is all I've known. Releasing the pain gives me a new perspective and gives me the opportunity to make different decisions for my life. The release is freeing in itself. Release comes in thoughts, understanding, and permission. When pain rises up, we can choose to say, "God thank you for showing me this pain I have been carrying, God I release it to you and take my hands off of it. Please help me to let go. God I am not sure how to do this, so please show me and I will walk with you, amen." Simple, honest prayers keep us accountable to ourselves that we are not in denial any longer and are truly desiring a new normal. It gives you the strength and courage to see yourself in a whole different light and from a fresh and new perspective. What you have released you can now leave with Jesus and walk away from the weight of it once and for all. Freedom is free, but It has requirements. In order for Jesus to be our savior, it cost Him something. In order for us to receive the freedom that comes with His sacrifice, we are required to accept and believe what He has done for us. Now we can have freedom and a fresh new start because we trusted God with what we have held dear to us, our wounds and ourselves.

What are you Feeling?

_____

_____

_____

_____

_____

_____

_____

_____

_____

CHAPTER *14*

Step 5: Learning To Forgive Others

---

*"...forgiving each other, just as in Christ God
forgave you"*
(Ephesians 4:32b).

This step can be hard. Sometimes my hurt seemed so deep that I could not conceive forgiving anyone that caused it. In some ways, I came to the false conclusion that by holding on to what someone did to me, I was hurting them in some way. I didn't understand that by not forgiving I was locked into the pain and remained at the point of the hurt. Forgiveness is a powerful release to the one forgiving. Choosing not to forgive is bondage to the one holding the grudge.

As I began to look over my life and think of the things I had endured, I came to the conclusion that by not forgiving those who hurt me I was paying them back for not protecting me in some way. I was angry at all those who made me feel like I wasn't wanted, needed or even worth being on this earth. I felt abandoned by those who were meant to be there for me and protect me. The anger towards schoolmates that tortured me daily and the teachers that made me feel insignificant or not good enough added to my pain. The feelings of abandonment, the lack of love, the lack of protection and the lack of appreciation were the chains around my neck and my heart. My hurt was covered by anger and my anger was covered by rage. Why was I born if everyone in my life only made me feel less than the person before them? Each person who hurt me, added more pain and wounds to my soul than the person before them. I asked myself over and over again., How could I ever be free from all this? I couldn't see a way out of it.

As I began to deal with my pain through church and a women's ministry, I started hearing about forgiveness. Someone telling me that I had to forgive someone who caused me so much pain and heartache made me angry. I felt they were continuing to get away with what they did to me. Forgiveness sounded to me like another way for those who hurt me to win over me. My anger had become my friend and comfort. It was all I knew to protect me. Why did I have to let go of my protection? Why did I have to let them off the hook for years of making me feel worthless? I needed someone to tell me that it was their fault, and it was my right to feel the way I did about them. Yes, it was their fault but my right to feel this way and hold on to the anger was making me lose instead of win. They deserved to be hated because of their treatment towards me. My soul was screaming and my mind began to spin. Forgiving instead of hating meant I would feel vulnerable again. I had to ask myself if I was really ready to release everything that had held me hostage since I was a child or did I want to remain in pain? My decision, as hard as it was, was that I wanted peace. Peace would only come by releasing my anger and hurt and beginning to forgive.

Forgiveness doesn't mean that the person or persons who hurt me didn't do anything. It didn't mean that I excused them from their part in my wounds. It meant that I could take back my power that they stole from me. Forgiveness is a gift to self. It is not enough to say out of your mouth that you forgive someone primarily because you feel you're expected to as a Christian or because it sounds like a great idea. Forgiveness is a process and it begins in the heart. It is felt in the heart and spirit before it ever comes through the lips. All the steps spoken of before this chapter is the process leading up to forgiveness. In order to know myself, I had to find out who I was holding on to in anger within myself. By doing so, I could discover the root of some of my anger, hurt and animosity so I could begin to heal. Take your time with the process of forgiveness. To bring up the people who hurt you means bringing up the pain of what was done. I was and I still am in a place in life where the freedom of forgiveness means more than holding baggage and pain from the past. The moments when I felt a release within my heart and spirit because I had moved beyond what they did to me felt like waves of calm, that hadn't been there before. Out of everything I have done in this process of self-discovery, forgiveness made me feel powerful. You must come to a place in life where you get to the root of the bitterness so you can ride the wave of forgiveness.

Going through the process of forgiving others can seem like you are climbing a rope. When you first begin, you feel strong and pull yourself up quickly. Then the thoughts, memories and faces of the people who brought hurt into your life begin to replay inside of you like a lion and you become fearful. You may become angry and begin to lose your strength to climb. Then you feel God's love giving you strength to keep going and again you begin to climb. The inner strength from God over shadows the fear of the memories and the anger. God's love gives you the strength to forgive and release all that is attached to their acts and words. You soon find yourself at the finish line and standing in the winning circle of Forgiveness. It is a win because each time we choose to forgive others we win. We gain strength. We gain victory.

You never have to speak to the person who abused you, betrayed you, tortured you or didn't protect you just because you forgive them. Should you choose to, you can do it knowing they no longer have power over you. You took it all back through forgiving them. Sometimes you don't realize you have forgiven someone until you see them or speak to them. This has happened to me many times. I was surprised that seeing them, hearing them, hearing about them, didn't cause my skin to crawl or my mind to become anxious as it normally would. In those moments the little girl within me became a strong and powerful woman. The acts against us silenced us, stole our voice and our ability to say no. Yet, through forgiveness we regain it all. It is a power move. It is a self-care move. It is a huge part of healing. Again, this part of the process will not only bring up the pain but the rage and fear attached to it. With each pull of the rope and each step taken on the stairs, you regain inner power, your inner voice and the noose around your wrist, feet and hands, fall to the floor.

What are you Feeling?

_____

_____

_____

_____

_____

_____

_____

_____

_____

CHAPTER *15*

Step 6: Choosing To Forgive Yourself

This is by far my hardest obstacle. Forgiving others takes time. However; forgiving yourself was unheard of for me. I didn't realize that finding myself would require me to dig so deep within. As I began to really look at who I was, I began to feel a lot of guilt about my decisions in my relationships, my decisions in how I lived my life and wondering why I made some of them. Those choices caused so much pain for me and it was embarrassing. As parts of my life replayed in my heart, mind and soul the guilt of my decisions were in the forefront of my life. I remembered when I attended the women's ministry many years ago and they talked about forgiveness it was hard to swallow. When they would teach about forgiving yourself, my first thought was "I didn't do anything so why do I need forgiveness?" I had to take responsibility for some of my life problems and also let go of the guilt of things that others did to me. The same steps that it takes to forgive others need to also be taken to forgive ourselves. Often times the steps to forgiving oneself are even greater because it requires self-inventory. We have fought to not look at ourselves and do an examination of self. In doing so, we again have to take responsibility for what we find in our time of examination. If you are anything like me, it may cause you to want to end the whole process.

My journey to self-discovery opened so many closed doors within me but I was determined this time I would not run away from what I uncovered. The closed doors represented the rooms within me that I learned to shut off from others, myself and even God in order to survive. These rooms had great stories that I never planned to revisit. Yet, this time I was determined I would not run away from what I uncovered. When I made the decision to do whatever I had to do as a child to get love, I made that decision from a desperate and fearful place. It was sheer desperation to feel wanted, appreciated and loved. That decision as I spoke of earlier caused a lifetime of pain. Yet when I wanted to discover why all my relationships with men were the same, the root of my choice had to be acknowledged. I needed to take responsibility for my choices. The truth that I needed to forgive myself for not knowing any better became clear.

The way I acknowledge what others had done to me was the way I needed to acknowledge what I had done to myself through desperation. The guilt was eating me up inside and bringing anger with it. By being honest with myself I understood that I was holding myself bound by my past. The chains around my neck were held by those I hadn't forgiven, including myself. It was not my fault that others didn't know how to love me. I couldn't change their heart or mind about loving an innocent child. They ignited

111

a need within me that set me in position to do what I thought was the only thing to do, look for love in others. I forgave myself for giving my body and mind as ransom for something they could never pay for, my self-worth and value. By doing this, I paid a price with my soul and spirit. I lost myself trying to find love in the wrong places. Even as I sit here and write, I am choosing to forgive the person I became. My soul no longer has a price that any human being can pay for. Jesus paid it all for me according to Mathew 20:28. The freedom of forgiveness is my gift to myself. Excusing what I've done in life is no longer an option to me. I decided to accept the truth. Being truthful with myself is a part of my journey to discover the real me. God has forgiven me and therefore I must forgive me (1 John 1:9). The search for love has ended because God shows me that He has always loved me with an everlasting love (Jeremiah 31:3). My heart became closed to Gods' love because I saw God as any other man. Therefore, there was no way He could love me honestly.

Forgiveness releases me from the shame that some of my choices brought. It is a genuine love for self. It allows you to unshackle yourself from lies and come face to face with the truth. It gives you the courage to say, "Yes that is who I was and that is what I did, but it is not who I was birthed to become." The more my pain and past would open up to me, the more I chose to face it. The more the lion roared, the more I took his strength by facing him and not running away. The more the pain was revealed, the more I began to see the real me behind the eyes that was once only filled with disgust and pain.

It's almost like seeing friends from high school who knew you were a certain way and now you are different. They want to keep reminding you of how you used to be and you want them to see the new you. When we don't forgive ourselves, we are the old friend of our own history. We still see ourselves as what we have done and who we were because guilt is there. Through forgiveness we can begin to see that change has come and we don't have to walk covered in shame anymore. It is beautiful to see yourself blossoming before your eyes by accepting that your past does not have to be your present or your future. It is empowering to see yourself brand new and know that each moment you release guilt that you can take another step of freedom and deliverance. You see the light come into your eyes that had been hidden before.

Forgiveness is transforming. When God forgave our sins, it allowed us to move from slavery and bondage to freedom and deliverance. By choosing to forgive ourselves we step out of chains into a crown of glory. I never knew all these years that I was holding myself captive. I blamed everyone else for all my pain and hardship. Yes, there were others responsible but in order to find my true self I needed to own my truth. Owning my truth opened the door that says my captivity as well as my freedom was in my hands. I realized that I had become comfortable in my pain because it was all I knew. Forgiving myself says that I can have a new comfort. I chose to receive the comfort and love that came with releasing myself from my own prison and walking in freedom. Each time I remembered something and dealt with everything that came with it, I chose to forgive me because I knew the freedom it would give. I believe the great gift is loving myself for who I am with all my flaws. The love that God gives me allows me to embrace my flaws and still love me. God knew I was flawed and He sent His Son Jesus to cover my sins through His blood and wash me clean {Mathew 1:21, Revelation 1:5}. There is no greater love than to give your only begotten son for the sins of Lynette {John 15:13}. By forgiving my sins, He protected me, loved me and made me brand new. I need to extend that same forgiveness to myself and this is what I continue to do daily.

What are you Feeling?

_____

_____

_____

_____

_____

_____

_____

_____

_____

CHAPTER *16*

Step 7: Be Comfortable With Being Okay

---

*"Thou wilt keep him in perfect peace, whose mind is
stayed on thee: because he trusteth in thee"*
(Isaiah 26:3 KJV).

Who would ever believe that it is easier to be at ease
with turmoil and chaos than to be at peace with
being okay? Turmoil and chaos were my constant
companions in life. When I began to see my life change,
peace was something new. One day I realized when
everything was calm and silent in my spirit it made me
uncomfortable and nervous. I would wonder what was
going on and try to analyze it. When I felt stressed or
overwhelmed I didn't even think to analyze what I was
feeling. It may sound crazy and in fact it felt crazy. God
showed me my pain and the discomfort that came with it
had become my friend. When you see things or people as
friends, you do not see them as a threat so you are not
trying to push them away. You are wanting to hold them
close. I needed to shift my mindset and perspective on

what I came to know as my friend and begin to see it as a foe. This was not an easy feat.

When I was in peace I could hear God and feel His presence. I loved that feeling because I felt protected and safe. God used one of those moments to reveal to me that I had become so comfortable with the chaos that I rejected peace. This was an eye opener to me. Can you really be so comfortable with dysfunction that peace is a foreign concept? Yes, you can and I had done just that.

I gave myself permission to want more for my life. I had to also give myself permission to be comfortable with being okay. We can become desensitized with goodness when all we have had is bad. We can become afraid of what protects us when all we have had is abandonment. It was an amazing day when God showed this to me. When I was at peace, I would question what I was feeling because I couldn't get settled within. The day God gave this wisdom to me, I gave myself the permission to be okay with being okay and to be comfortable with it. I had to learn a new normal. That normal is peace. It sure feels better than chaos but learning to just rest in it and accept it, required baby steps.

The journey of life is a daily birth to life changing moments. In an instant you can be fearful and in the next brave. Peace is my life changing moment. Being okay with me is a life changing moment. Accepting that I am not perfect and I never have to be is a life changing moment. I can take a deep breath. I'm resting in peace through that deep breath and it allows my mind and soul to trust God and be comfortable. The process of letting go and receiving from God such a great love brings up many questions and they are settled in His Peace.

We don't have to understand the peace He gives us because His Word says it will surpass our understanding (Phil. 4:7). We have searched for love and it was always there. We have had our lives filled with anger, hurt, abandonment, fear and heartbreak. Through life we will feel those emotions again, sometimes more intensely. Giving ourselves permission to rest in the peace of God, guarantees that even when we go through them, our rest is in His peace.

My spirit, my heart, my mind and my soul have my permission to say, "I find my rest in the freedom of being okay." Something so simple becomes so terrifying when you don't know any better. I am so thankful to God for the moment when He showed me I needed a new normal. My heart filled with such love from Him. He not only was changing who I had become from the inside out, He was teaching me to rest in it. He was in that moment my protector. He protected me from the deceptions of Satan blinding me of the fact that when I thought I was in turmoil within, that I was really safe in the Lord.

You must give yourself the permission to be okay. You must trust God to be okay. Transition is not easy. The progress that we make daily is a moment of triumph. If we only see how far we have to go, we can never be okay with the moments in between. Look at how far you have come. Look at what you have survived. When we give ourselves permission to be okay, we give ourselves permission to not only live but also to thrive.

What are you Feeling?

_____

_____

_____

_____

_____

_____

_____

_____

_____

_____

PART 3

CHAPTER 17

Mindset Shift Baby Girl

"...but be ye transformed by the renewing of your mind"
(Romans 12:2).

I have found the hardest part of change is to shift the mind. The thoughts we have are based on what we were taught, what we have gone through and our understanding now about ourselves and life. As we have walked the journey of self-discovery, we are tearing down old ways and lies we believed as truth. Breakthrough is possible. Overcoming is available. Renewing our mind is necessary.

The mind is powerful. It is no less powerful as we peel back layers of our life and deal with the layers of pain beneath the masks. The mind holds stories and our subconscious never sleeps. The mind is where we can have the greatest struggle on our journey. We can desire new and speak new, but if we don't shift our mind, all we will have is old. Just like we work hard to become physically fit, it is imperative that we work to become mentally fit. As with any change, we must acknowledge how we think about ourselves and the things we have been through. As we examine our thoughts, we can find our source of being stuck. Our mind will lead us, move us, derail us or make us feel like failures. The thoughts in our mind create images that bring shame, pain and silence. Our mind needs new food, so we can eat healthy. If our minds are sick with negative thoughts and images, we will speak negative and sick words to ourselves.

In Matthew 9:20-21 in The New King James Version of the bible says, "For she said to herself, if only I may touch His garment, I shall be made well." There were many words inside her own mind she had to push through to get to this place. For 12 years she fought ridicule and abandonment from those around her. I believe her biggest struggle was not the outward ridicule, but the inward ridicule and shame. She pushed through her old thoughts. She pushed through her need for approval or affirmation. She pushed through what she knew about herself and her situation to get to a new Word because she shifted her mind. She realized The Word was walking by and He was The Word that would heal every word within her that she was fighting. She repeated to herself something that forced what she originally had been saying to herself to die away. She repeated the same words until she BELIEVED THEM. The battle of the mind is torturous. The old thoughts are not only of the things you have fought through, but it is a reminder of how you felt regarding them. Just like the woman with the issue of blood, your flow of feeling insignificant, alone and unworthy must come to a place where they are at your feet and no longer hindering you from pushing forward.

Even as I write these words, my journey of shifting my mind continues. The shift is continuous. There are thoughts that are hidden in the corners of your mind that are old. They push daily to pull you into the norm. Those thoughts are fighting diligently when God has called you to walk through a door that may seem uncomfortable and fearful. The new information you receive to change your life is wrestling with the old thoughts. You are the one who must decide which thoughts will be a part of your life today. Your growth and continuation of walking in your healing will shift you and shake the foundation within you that was all you knew until you decided to cry out to God, "Help Me."

Do you realize the power you gain by using your power of choice to go in search of you? To heal your inner, painful wounds? take another step? live beyond the painful circumstances of your life? Your choice will never cease to have power, so use it wisely. The foundation you have stood on has become shaky underneath your feet. You may feel unstable because things around and within may feel as if you are falling apart. It is in your mind where the perception of your life changing must shift. It is a beautiful experience to see where I was and where I am. Along the way I felt as if I was reverting in some way to how I knew myself and how I felt about myself. What I discovered is, the moments of battle required my choice and my attention. Even though I was healing, my mind has memories. Today we can rely on God who says we are to have a mind like His. His mind is perfect, and He says we can think on what is holy and pure. So even though you may not feel steady, know that you are right where you are purposed to be.

Begin to speak to yourself in kindness, love, truth and hope. Your words plant seeds in the ground of your mind, heart and soul. As you change your language, you change your life. As you change your words you create new memories for your mind to absorb and replay back to you in the same way your stories of pain did repeatedly for years. Your words create a road map to where you are going. What do you want your life to represent to the world now? What do you want to bring to the table now? Create it with your thoughts and your words. We have told ourselves for so long we were victims because of the pages of our story. We learned to live in the old neighborhood of "victim hood" and we have been evicted. We can only return to the familiar place of turmoil if we choose to. I don't know about you, but the more I learn about myself, the less I desire to choose my old neighborhood. The more my eyes become clear and I could see how my mind can take me into amazing places based on what I fed it, I became more determined to push through and burn the door to my old neighborhood. It no longer fed me. It no longer spoke my language. We must be determined to STOP repping our old to STAND in the NEW. We must STOP repping hurt, fear, pain, what was, or can't. Our new language and mentality must become, I CAN, I AM,

ABUNDANCE, PURPOSE, DREAM, VISIONARY, MORE THAN ENOUGH, CONFIDENT, MINDSET SHIFT and OVERCOMER. You can't LIVE in a NEW HOUSE with the old Neighborhood Mentality.

Look at it this way. The woman with the issue of blood touched Jesus hem and she was made whole. She was healed. She allowed her faith to take her in a direction contrary to where her pain held her. In doing so, she received what she never had, healing. Had she gotten up from her place of healing and gone right back to her place of brokenness, she could blame only herself. There was something about the touch that separated her new self from her old self. Her old clothes were covered in fifth. Her new clothes were covered in glory. To try and go back into our old neighborhood with the brightness of glory will make you feel that you belong in the place of filth. The glory ignites the potent smell of the old, ragged clothes and you recognize you are in the wrong place. To follow though where healing is taking you, the removal of the old clothes becomes necessary, because they no longer fit. The woman with the issue of blood is a representation of all women in some way. Many of us have been in pain so deep and so long, that we are on the ground and can drag ourselves to the feet of Jesus. As the woman with the "Issues" for twelve long years came to recognize something greater than her past clothing and state of mind, so can we. She began to speak to herself over and over the words that caused a shift in her mind, her perspective and her position. As we use our mind to shift us and allow our words to move us, our perspective, position and our mind evolves. It helps us to recognize where we are, who's are and where we can go.

There are thoughts that are hidden in the corners of your mind, that are old. They will strive daily to pull you into what is the norm. God has called you to walk through a door that may seem uncomfortable and fearful. Yet, when you trust God with the uncomfortable places within you, He will fortify your mind to enter the new territory. He will allow it to become your new norm. Believe in yourself and believe in God within you. Change is inevitable for PROGRESS to happen. You GOT THIS GIRL. So, go forth with a FORTIFIED mind.

Baby Girl, the power is in your hands. What is it you shall begin to repeatedly speak to yourself? What are you going to repeatedly think to yourself? You have touched the hem of Jesus and your issues have ceased to control you and torture you with memories of defeat. God has shifted you. Get up and walk. Get up and move from where you thought your feet could never leave and your feet would never allow you to go. Get up!

Take up your bed and walk baby girl.

What are you Feeling?

CHAPTER 18

Believe Baby Girl

---

*"Jesus said unto him, 'If thou canst believe, all
things are possible to him that believeth'"*
(Mark 9:23).

Take a deep breathe. Release. Move

You are here in this space where you have only
dreamed of or believed it was for someone else. The space
where you get to Believe Different than what your life
experiences told you. Yes, it is possible, and it is possible
for you. By going through this journey of searching and
finding you, you are learning to believe in the impossible.
As your vision clears and your mind clears, you can move
into a rebirth.

God has seen your life and He knew one day you would
hunger for more. First the baggage of what was, had to be
released from your life. As a plane rising into the clouds, it
can only do so when it carries a certain weight. The
captain decides something must go when the weight

exceeds the limitation. He releases what may seem valuable to passengers, their luggage. In doing so, the plane can further ascend into the clouds without the plane falling to the ground. You are the captain of your life and you get to decide what weight you have been carrying that has been holding you down to the ground and hindering your ascension into more. You have been holding on to baggage of the voices that told you, you could not and would not be anything. The baggage of unspoken pain and broken pieces refused to allow you to get off the ground.

Now, your journey is allowing you to breathe. With every breath you are reborn. With every breath you are relaunching the very thing inside you that you believed was without life. Every time you choose to release yourself and your belongings (thoughts, ideas, visions, disappointment, etc.) to God, your load is lessened, and now you can SOAR.

One of the great lessons learned in my journey is all the experiences, the disappointments and my search for truth is purposed. Yes, all of it. Each part of my journey, not just the good parts, were steps in life to get me to right now. I needed each step. I needed each moment. I needed each rejection. I needed the fear and insecurity because it all built me into the woman I have and shall become. I believe without those steps you would not have been hungry or thirsty to live. You may think with everything you have gone through, it could not possibly have a purpose in it. You may believe at some point you almost took your life because life became unbearable, I did. You may believe at some point you were so low to the ground that you felt you were underneath it, I did. As valid as all these experiences are, I encourage you to change your perspective and see them as steps in the light of your Destiny. Each experience, at the time, could have taken your ability to live and the desire to get up, but it didn't. Each time you became paralyzed by fear and pain, you could have given up on anything ahead of you being better. At an appointed time, your hunger and thirst began to increase for more. At an appointed time, you refused to accept ultimatums and you began your search for what would not only quench your thirst and hunger but satisfy them in a way nothing else could compare.

Breathe Baby Girl....

You are moving. You are elevating. You are here. In all the rubble of your life, you found the strength to push through and show your hands to the world. As the dirt of life poured upon you, you lifted your hand. Imagine a seed being planted under the soil. Imagine concrete being poured over grass. There is a seed planted underneath and it is purposed to live and live it shall. Yes, it needs water. Yes, it needs sun. Yes, for such a time as this, it needs to be planted, but live it shall. Somewhere along the way, no matter what covered that seed, it begins to push through the dirt and stretch through the cracks and begins to ascend. It knows it is purposed to sprout but everything around it tells it to deny what is within this lonesome seed. The circumstances surrounding it says, "you only get to go this far." Yet, the purpose shall not be denied. Your purpose shall not be denied. The experiences and struggles you have endured says, "you only get to go this far." God says, "For such a time as this, you shall live and live abundantly."

Yes, you. Your journey to self brought you back to your seed of purpose within. The rage will cease. The fiery words will be covered in love. The veil over your eyes has been removed. Will it be perfect? Certainly not. Your journey will always have another step. Your journey will always have a dark place where you look up and see the light ahead, but you have a reference of overcoming that you can relate to and grab strength from. Your stairs may look insurmountable, but you can refer to your journey to uncover who you are really to remind you that you can take another step.

The light is drawing you to each new level of your life. The life you have been purposed to live despite the surroundings, is calling you. Despite what is covering you, there is always life within you ready to be birthed. You have everything within you to continue to peel back new levels and layers within you. The more you grow, the more layers you will uncover. Remember the dirt. Remember the concrete. Remember the life that springs through it.

Breathe Baby Girl

Rise to the occasion. Stand in your light. Breathe your air. Dance to your beat. Embrace Now. Your pain is no longer the only voice speaking to you. It no longer holds a high regard for you. Your pain has purpose and has fed your hunger. Now believe the voice you received in your search has always been within you pushing to be heard. The laughter you hear, is the childlike laughter buried under abuse and rejection, waiting for your hunger for it to be greater than the pain that silenced it. You went back to the place that caused your turmoil and spoke life to it. You are the sunshine and the water the little girl within you needed. You told her she was destined for greatness. You took her hand as she stood on the step below you looking for someone to help her up. Now you are one. The sister standing on the step above you, is the part of you waiting for you to grow into her. She is reaching down for you, take her hand.

Breathe Baby Girl and MOVE...

The same God who heard your cry for help is shifting your story. Believe in you. Believe in God. Your story has started a new chapter. It may not all be clear, but know God is with you. No longer do you have to wait for the knight on the white horse to come and rescue you. The one who placed the knight on the horse is your knight in amour. No one can tear Him down, no one can defeat Him, and in Him, you are safe. God is restoring your belief system in Him. You placed your belief in so many who were incapable of answering your deep cry of pain. Yet, God says, "Forgive and let go." They were purposed to answer your call when they did because they deepened your hunger for Truth. They deepened your thirst for wholeness. Believe in the lessons you learned each time you were let down and disappointed. Believe in the lessons you received each time you felt your heart was shattered. The lessons are serving you even now. Your story is shifting, and you shall know true love. Now you shall give from your overflow.

Breathe Baby Girl and LIVE..

I applaud you for finding the courage to go in search of the woman you were meant to be before life happened. The woman God knew you would be before the first wound was inflicted and you cried your first tear of abandonment. The woman you thought never existed, can now walk free in boldness and confidence. The desire and need to attach to those who have allowed their wounds to ooze onto you because they are wrapped in bandages of their own is no longer with you. Now you can recognize the wounded, but in a different way. You now have the capacity to pray for those who wounded you and who may never ask for your forgiveness. Through Gods' love within you, you know you can live on even though they never apologize to you, because you are safe. You did this for you. You gave yourself permission to Believe in you for the first time in your life and I applaud you. You Believed in an invisible Father and now you can hold His hand without fear, shame and silence. You have been set free.

As you continue to walk out your healing, believe you can move forward with vitality, hope, focus and elegance. Your walk is graceful. Your words are loving toward yourself and others. Your steps are ordered of the Lord and you move with assurance that God sees you and He always has. Nothing will ever change that.

Breathe Baby Girl and RISE..

What are you Feeling?

_____

_____

_____

_____

_____

_____

_____

_____

CHAPTER 19

Time To Embrace Love

"A time to love…" (Ecclesiastes 3:8a).

Embrace according to the dictionary means to hug, clasp or hold close to the bosom. As God was bringing me into a new life, my heart was changing. I could feel love from Him and I loved the way it made me feel. I can now embrace love and hold it close to my heart because now I know it is mine and always has been. By embracing love I was embracing God who is Love. Each time God reveals more of me to me, He is teaching me that I deserve to be loved. My life situations had taken that knowledge from me. Now I can see that regardless of my shame, my pain, my wounds I was created in love, by love and for love. Hosea 4:6 says, "My people perish from a lack of knowledge." The knowledge that I never received was causing the person I was created to be to perish. Having that knowledge was causing my heart to open up and feel. It amazes me how taking hold of something that was a lie, became real. In order to receive love, I had to do the same thing. Embracing what was held back from me would also give me the self-esteem and confidence that was hidden within me. I would find myself smiling to myself and just feeling so good inside. Who am I? That question was continuing to evolve and widen as I began to see myself differently. All the steps that God had shown me to get to this point has taken time. When I came to the point of being ready to embrace who I am, time stood still.

Embracing love brought about wisdom within me. Even though I was embracing love there were those small areas within me that said, "Why would God want to love someone like me?" I felt that I was damaged goods and not able to be used by God for anything. God was teaching me that He knew who I was called to be before I was born (Jeremiah 1:5). My life journey didn't change His purpose for my life. The damage caused by the past, shall be used for Gods' glory. Everything endured would be used to bring others into the knowledge of their worth and value. This was true for me and it is surely true for you. Knowing this made me feel excited that I could help someone else. To me that meant that I was being healed not only for me but for the other women and girls who need to know that they deserve to be loved. God's love feels like a continuous hug. He saw me as being worthy enough for that love even after everything that made me look dirty in my eyes. Yes, I wanted to embrace love because now I knew that I was embracing God.

When others abuse us in any way, it causes our self-esteem to crouch down. When we are meant to be loved and we are not, it causes our confidence to crouch down. The desperation to get what we deserve causes our spirit to break under the pressure of using human means to deal with spiritual pain. Gods' love fills those empty spaces. Through the circumstances of life, we run from *Gods'* love. His love feels uncomfortable as it touches the broken pieces of who we are. We have compared Gods' love to the illusion of love others can and have given us. By choosing to no longer run from that love, but instead turning to it, we are saying, "I no longer see you as a foe- but goodness for me, and I accept you."

The steps that I have shared with you are only a few that have helped me along my journey to finding myself. Embracing love brings peace to my rage. It brings clarity to my confusion. It brings healing to my pain. The search for love has ended and each day I have to remind myself that I no longer need to search in others for what I have discovered in God for me. The person looking back at me in the mirror now has beautiful brown eyes that some days still shed tears but they also shine with joy.

We have been through so many situations in life that made us feel anything but loved. We had our innocence stolen. We had our self-esteem tormented. We covered our wounds with rage. We placed one mask upon another to cover who we really are. Love will pull back the many layers of the mask so that we can breathe. I am beautiful and so are you. I am creative and so are you. I am loved and so are you. Under the pressure of the mask my truth was hidden. Love caused it to be revealed. Love gave me life. Some days I feel like a flower blossoming and I can literally see a rose opening up beautifully under the rays of the sun. The sun shining on me is the Father pouring His love upon my heart and causing it to come into its' purpose and truth. I never knew that love could be so powerful. More importantly I didn't know that Love would make me feel so powerful and beautiful.

What is hiding under that mask that we use daily? The makeup we cover up with to look good to the world. The best clothes that we wear to impress those that see us. Underneath all that is a wounded child who needs love. God is waiting for us to embrace Him. He is waiting patiently for us to desire to know our true authentic self and worth. Remember the flower blossoming and know that is you and me. Our season has changed and it is our time to hold love close to our bosom because it belongs to us. We have been hidden too long under the might of pain and now the Love of God is here to walk us into our purpose, our worth, our value and self-love.

Love uncovers what fear held captive. 1 John 4:18 says;

There is no fear in love; but perfect love casteth out fear.

Love develops that which was lying dormant within us. Sit still, take a deep breath, open your heart and welcome love in. You have purpose and destiny waiting for you to step into love. No longer do you need to search for people and/or things to fill the void within. You are the child that God has always loved. Your time to allow that love to show you who you really are is now. Open your arms and welcome it in.

What are you Feeling?

CHAPTER *20*

The Journey Continues

---

*"And we know that all things work together for good
to them that love God, to them who are the called
according to his purpose"*
(Romans 8:28).

My search of finding myself has been painful, fearful
and eye opening. Each day that God reveals more to
me, I realize that He is preparing me to help other women
who don't know their worth, value or have self-love. It's
amazing to me that God can take what others see in our
lives as nothing and use it in such a mighty way. What we
have endured in life is the vehicle God can use to birth into
us Greatness.

All the heartache, the disappointment and the obstacles
have put us into the birthing position to birth our Destiny
and purpose. It is all working for our good now (Romans
8:28). God will use our mess and our masks to unveil
hidden treasures within us under the rubble of shame and
fear. My soul gives birth to Wisdom as God speaks within

me. He gives me the courage daily to not give up. Being able to see myself as worth something becomes more real to me daily. When you feel you aren't worth anything, you accept any type of treatment from others and yourself. The parts of my body that others called ugly over the years are daily becoming beautiful to me because of Gods' love.

Who am I? I am a woman of God. I am a mother. I am friend. I am sister. I am a writer. I am ministry. I am purposed. I am brave. I am strong. I am beautiful. I am anointed. I am destined for greatness. This is who I am and more. This is the same woman who for 40 plus years thought she was not good enough or worth anything. When I found the strength to answer the question, "Who am I," I never knew what I would find. I found me through Christ and my discovery is not over. I still have labor pains of letting go of the old me and embracing the new me. Those labor pains as before are causing me to bear down and push because there is a spiritual child within me waiting to be birthed into my life.

What will it take for us to be sick and tired of being this illusion of ourselves? At what point in our life will we choose to stop running to and fro looking to others to validate us and make us feel special? I would say now is a great time to stop in your tracks and face yourself in the mirror. God has made you accepted in the beloved according to Ephesians 1:6. He loves us so much that He accepted us knowing what we would go through, what decisions we would make and the roads we would take. He accepted us. Knowing this, gives us the power of knowing that we don't need anyone to validate us. Validate means to approve. We already have the approval of God.

Life is a journey not a goal to cross a finish line. As long as we are alive it is another day to choose to look within ourselves-- underneath who we had to become to survive-- and discover the amazing person that we are. There is a person waiting to be discovered and that person is you. The first step is to ask yourself, "Who am I" and then be open to discovery. Life will give us many labor pains. God will give us the wisdom to know when it is time to push. He will also give us the strength to just breathe as the labor pains become more intense. God wants His children to discover the hidden gem within.

You have found the courage to begin without even realizing it. You opened the cover to this book because somewhere inside you there is a cry to open the package that holds your truth. It has been held back from you for so long. You are brave. You are loved. You are Courageous and you are worth it. The journey continues and it is the most amazing journey every taken. No more do we need others to define or validate us according to how they see us. When we begin to open the truth of who we are and find our identity in Christ, the masks begin to crumble to the ground. We are finding ourselves through Gods love for us that has come to rescue and restore us. Take a seat. Take a deep breath. Close your eyes and ask yourself, "Who am I" and go in search of you.

What are you Feeling?

CONCLUSION

AFFIRMATIONS: a statement or proposition that is declared to be true.

As we change our language, we can struggle to shift our mind, change our natural inner language. Affirmations daily speak to my mind and I want to share with you some affirmations you can use to assist you on your journey into the woman you are becoming. As you read each affirmation, make it personable and put your name in front of each. Write these affirmations and any others you choose and put them on your mirror. Say them to yourself over and over and over until you believe them for yourself.

1. I Am Enough
2. I Am Loved
3. I Am Necessary
4. I Am Authentic
5. I Am Healed
6. I Live in Gods' Abundance for my life
7. I Walk by Faith and Not by Sight
8. I Am More Than I Have Believed
9. I Am Purposed for Greatness
10. I Am The Righteousness of God
11. I Am Capable & Equipped To Do Whatever I Need To Do
12. I Have a Renewed Mind
13. I Am Blessed to be a Blessing
14. I Am Brave

15. I Am Strong
16. I Am Significant
17. I Am Love
18. I Am Truth
19. I Have a Sound Mind
20. I Am a Warrior
21. I Am Surrounded by people God Has Divinely Connected To Me To Live In and On Purpose
22. I Attract Love
23. I Attract Truth
24. I Attract Blessings
25. I Am Physically Fit
26. I Am Emotionally Fit
27. I Am Mentally Fit
28. I Am Joy

ABOUT THE AUTHOR

Lynette M Bradshaw began writing many years ago for her former church as she discovered her gift of writing through God's leading. It wasn't until many years later, she began to write for herself as a way of dealing with heartache in her search for love and acceptance and the desire to heal her negative view of Self. Lynette is also the author of, In Search of Me-The Workbook, Moments of Gratitude Journal (Companion Journal for In Search of Me) The Locked Chamber: Healing The Hearts of God's Daughters. She is a Transformational Speaker, Coach & Photographer. She is a graduate of Louisiana Business college and Medvance Institute and currently works in the medical field as a Medical Assistant.

When she is not writing, she can be found enjoying photography, spending time with her children, dancing and exercising.

Pick up a copy of the companion Workbook (In Search of Me-The Workbook) and Moments of Gratitude-Journal for In Search of Me at www.Amazon.com or www.RestoreHerWorth.com

Contact Information

Website: www.RestoreHerWorth.com

Email: Lynette@RestoreHerWorth.com

Facebook: http://bit.ly/LynetteMBradshaw

YouTube:

https://tinyurl.com/LynetteMBradshawLive